D1575377

Columbia University

Contributions to Education

Teachers College Series

No. 802

AMS PRESS
NEW YORK

THE PREVENTION OF FAILURE
IN FIRST GRADE READING
By Means of Adjusted Instruction

By HOWARD THOMAS DUNKLIN

SUBMITTED IN PARTIAL FULFILLMENT OF THE
REQUIREMENTS FOR THE DEGREE OF DOCTOR
OF PHILOSOPHY IN THE FACULTY OF PHI-
LOSOPHY, COLUMBIA UNIVERSITY

Published with the Approval of
Professor Arthur I. Gates, Sponsor

Bureau of Publications
Teachers College · Columbia University
New York · 1940

Library of Congress Cataloging in Publication Data

Dunklin, Howard Thomas, 1899-
    The prevention of failure in first grade reading by
means of adjusted instruction.

    Reprint of the 1940 ed., issued in series: Teachers
College, Columbia University. Contributions to educa-
tion, no. 802.
    Originally presented as the author's thesis, Columbia.
    Bibliography: p.
    1. Reading (Primary) 2. Reading--Ability testing.
I. Title. II. Series: Columbia University. Teachers
College. Contributions to education, no. 802.
LB1573.D78 1972   372.4'14   71-176733

ISBN 0-404-55802-X

Reprinted by Special Arrangement with Teachers
College Press, New York, New York

From the edition of 1940, New York
First AMS edition published in 1972
Manufactured in the United States

AMS PRESS, INC.
NEW YORK, N. Y.   10003

LB 1573
·D 78
copy 1

ACKNOWLEDGMENTS

Most educational research depends for its success upon the cooperation of many people in various capacities. The writer of the present research study was particularly fortunate in the quality and amount of cooperation he received.

The Dissertation Committee gave invaluable assistance in the planning of the research and in the presentation of the report. With deep appreciation, the writer acknowledges his debt to Professor Arthur I. Gates for constant encouragement and guidance in the orientation of the study with other work in the field. Professor Lois C. Mossman contributed much to broaden the writer's concept of the reading process in relation to the learner. Professor Henry A. Ruger made valuable suggestions relative to statistical treatment and organization.

The research was carried on in the public schools of Buffalo, New York. The writer is especially indebted to Harriet Butler, Supervisor of Primary Grades in that city. She aided in the selection of schools both by making available statistics of enrollment and promotion and by giving advice regarding personnel. Throughout the progress of the study, she helped greatly by supporting the project and by giving generously of her time for suggestions and encouragement. The heads of the Department of Extension Education, Supervisor George E. Smith, M.D., and Director R. Pratt Krull (now Associate Superintendent), encouraged the writer throughout the research. They made available the services of a school psychologist.

For advice as to selection of teachers and for administrative assistance the writer is grateful to Mabel M. Brogan, Principal of Stinson Primary School, to Harriet M. Bartow, Assistant Principal in Charge of School Number 5, and to Emma L. Lodge, Principal of School Number 74. A large measure of the credit for whatever of value has resulted from the research must go to the three teachers of the Experimental Group, Laura J. Minns, Dorothy C. Reichel, and Josephine A. Tauriello. The writer feels greatly indebted to the first grade children who participated in the experiment.

The careful and accurate testing done by Edna Benson Dunklin

iii

made possible well-matched experimental and control groups at the beginning of the experiment and insured a reliable record of the progress of these groups at its close.

Special acknowledgment is due Edward M. Durney, M.D., Director of Child Hygiene, Buffalo Board of Health, Melvin L. Belzer, M.D., William Howard, M.D., and Joseph C. O'Gorman, M.D., who conducted the physical examinations of children taking part in the experiment.

In the typing of the manuscript, Althea Baldwin's accuracy and thoroughness were invaluable.

The writer is especially grateful to his wife, Laura Dolan Dunklin, for her constant encouragement and assistance throughout the conduct of the research.

H. T. D.

CONTENTS

TABLES

CHAPTER I

A TENTATIVE PROGRAM OF ADJUSTMENT

THE large number of failures among beginners in reading has been increasingly a matter of concern both to the research worker and to the practical educator in the field. The success of instruction which is adjusted to the abilities and interests of these failing children suggests that many of them might have succeeded from the beginning had their first instruction been as well adjusted to their needs as the remedial teaching.

PLAN OF THE REPORT

The purpose of the present study is (1) to survey the literature concerned with primary reading with a view to developing a tentative program of adjusted instruction which would be practicable in an average schoolroom, (2) to test this tentative program experimentally in order to determine what degree of success would follow its application, and (3) to make the program available for use in further research and in educational practice.

The report of this study is addressed to two diverse groups—the research worker and the administrator or teacher. To a great extent, materials offered in the report which would be of most interest to the one would seem irrelevant or confusing from the point of view of the other. Accordingly, the first four chapters are written for the research worker: research background, procedure, treatment of data, and results. The Appendix is written for the teacher or administrator. The research worker who requires a more complete description of the materials and methods than is given in the second chapter will find it in the Appendix. The teacher or administrator who plans to adopt the materials and methods will, perhaps, desire to examine the more technical chapters to assure himself that the program was sufficiently successful to warrant its adoption. This plan of organization represents an effort toward shortening the lag between research and application deplored by scientists in education.[1]

[1] William S. Gray, "Need of Cooperation between Laboratory and Classroom," *Journal of Educational Research,* 29:484–485, February, 1936. Paul McKee,

THE NEED FOR A PROGRAM OF ADJUSTED INSTRUCTION IN READING

Adequate reading ability is essential both for the pupil's school success and for his emotional and social adjustment. Under prevailing conditions of instruction many children fail to achieve adequate reading ability. On the other hand, when instruction has been adjusted to the individual needs of the learners many children have been successful who almost certainly would have failed without this adjustment. Other children who have already failed have become successful when given remedial instruction adjusted to their needs.

The Importance of Reading Ability for School Success

The evidence of scientific studies corroborates the belief of teachers and administrators that school success depends upon reading ability. Percival[2] found that 99.15 per cent of the failures in first grade in the cities he studied were failures in reading. The percentage remained high in second and third grades. Lee[3] found that, in grades four, five, and six, those children whose reading ability fell below the fourth grade level on standard tests were almost certain to have unsatisfactory achievement in other subjects. For success in carrying on the reading activities expected of junior high school pupils, Gray[4] suggests that a grade score of at least 7.0 is necessary. Bond's[5] research indicates no such definite minimum of reading ability for successful achievement in junior high school work. She found, however, that in these grades better reading ability will be accompanied by better scholastic achievement.

The Importance of Reading Ability for Mental Health

Perhaps the most serious effects of failure to develop an adequate reading ability are the social maladjustments and distortion of personality which result. Typical of the cases reported by remedial teachers are the four which Blanchard[6] discusses. She observes that

"Problems of Research: An Evaluation," *Fourth Annual Research Bulletin*, pp. 25–30. National Conference on Research in Elementary School English, 1936.

[2] Walter P. Percival, *A Study of the Causes and Subjects of School Failure.* 1926.

[3] Doris M. Lee, *The Importance of Reading for Achieving in Grades Four, Five, and Six.* 1933.

[4] William S. Gray, "The Nature and Organization of Basic Instruction in Reading," *The Teaching of Reading: A Second Report*, pp. vii–442. 1937.

[5] Eva Bond, *Reading and Ninth Grade Achievement.* 1938.

[6] Phyllis Blanchard, "Reading Disabilities in Relation to Maladjustment," *Mental Hygiene*, 12:772–788, October, 1928.

failure in reading sets up feelings of inferiority in the individuals which lead to the development of personality and behavior aberrations unless adequate compensation is achieved. Among these aberrations are daydreaming, lack of interest, and oversensitivity to fancied slights. Monroe [7] also found from her analysis of cases that children who fail to learn to read may develop emotional and personality problems. Ladd [8] investigated the relationships between some personality traits and reading failure and found less pronounced differences between good and poor readers than other investigators have found. Monroe and Backus [9] found the following types of personality maladjustment among reading disability cases: aggression, withdrawal, compensation, defeat, and hypertension. They give reports from teachers which show that in general improvement in reading under remedial instruction is accompanied by a proportionate improvement in behavior.

Two reports have been selected to show how factors in the school and home environment operate to develop such distortions of personality in children whose attainment in reading fails to meet some expected standard. Mosher [10] describes the methods and results of teaching a class of twenty-six beginners by the "Look-and-Say" method. The class was divided into three groups. The rapid and the average groups made satisfactory progress. The C, or low group, read much less than the others, yet, at the end of the year, according to test results, they had failed to learn their small vocabulary as well as the A and B groups had learned their larger ones. In a class in which other children were enjoying a much greater success, these children of the C group are described as being noticeably lacking in interest and enthusiasm in matters pertaining to the activities of the school. In their withdrawal from the activities of the class, they evidenced the beginnings of social maladjustment.

The second report describes the effect upon children of their parents' attitudes toward their success. Henderson [11] found, in inter-

---

[7] Marion Monroe, *Children Who Cannot Read: The Analysis of Reading Disabilities and the Use of Diagnostic Tests in the Instruction of Retarded Readers*, pp. xvi–206. 1932.

[8] Margaret R. Ladd, *The Relation of Social, Economic, and Personal Characteristics to Reading Ability*, p. 100. 1933.

[9] Marion Monroe and Bertie Backus, *Remedial Reading*, pp. xi–171. 1937.

[10] R. M. Mosher, "Some Results of Teaching Beginners by the Look-and-Say Method," *Journal of Educational Psychology*, 19:185–193, March, 1928.

[11] B. M. Henderson, "Parental Attitudes toward First-Grade Achievement," *Understanding the Child*, 7:21–25, October, 1938.

views with one hundred mothers of first grade children, that, typically, mothers showed great concern when their children's progress in reading appeared to them to be slower than that of other children. Some parents insisted on home reading even though the children showed definite signs of fatigue. Some children showed concern and worry over the more rapid progress of their classmates. Typical of these children was the girl whose real interest in school changed to an unhappy anxiety. Another child read at every opportunity in the hope of learning to read as well as her friends. She developed a serious and unhappy appearance. Behavior such as Mosher and Henderson describe may easily develop into the more obvious types of personality maladjustment discussed by Monroe and Backus.

Frequency of Failure in First Grade

The importance of learning to read, both for success in school and for mental health, is well recognized. However, despite the efforts that have been made to improve methods and materials of teaching and thereby insure a greater degree of success in learning to read, many failures still occur. Pugsley,[12] discussing general trends, reports that from one-third to one-sixth of first grade children fail, and that 99 per cent of first grade failures are failures in reading. Otto[13] finds that the greatest percentage of failure occurs in first grade, and that reading is the subject in which most failures occur. Heck[14] finds, in studying reports from one hundred and twenty-five city school systems, that failure in first grade ranged from 7.2 per cent to 24 per cent, the median being 16.5 per cent. From their study of promotion practices in city school systems Mort and Featherstone[15] find an average of 20.1 per cent failure in low first and 8.4 per cent failure in high first grade.

Surveys of individual school systems reveal similar percentages of failure. According to a survey of Newburgh[16] schools in 1929 there was 60 per cent failure in grade 1. The report states that this abnormally high percentage probably results from the practice of ad-

[12] C. A. Pugsley, "Reducing and Handling Student Failures," *School Board Journal*, 86:18–20, March, 1933.
[13] Henry J. Otto, "Implications for Administration and Teaching Growing out of Pupil Failures in First Grade," *Elementary School Journal*, 33:25–32, September, 1932.
[14] Arch O. Heck, *Administration of Pupil Personnel*. 1929.
[15] Paul R. Mort and W. B. Featherstone, *Entrance and Promotion Practices in City School Systems: Standards and Accounting Procedures*. 1932.
[16] *Report of the Survey of the Schools of Newburgh, New York*. 1929.

mitting underage children directly to first grade rather than to kindergarten. A 1931 survey of the Pasadena [17] schools shows 11.5 per cent failure in 1B and 14.1 per cent failure in 1A. In 1932 a survey of Chicago's schools [18] indicated 17 per cent to 20 per cent failure in the first grade. An Alabama state survey of the Conecuh County [19] Schools in 1932 revealed that, of the children in first grade, 53.9 per cent were repeaters. In 1935, according to a survey of the Evansville [20] schools there was, in the first semester, 16.6 per cent failure in 1B and 19.4 per cent in 1A; and in the second semester, 12.2 per cent failure in 1B and 4.8 per cent in 1A. The reports of such surveys indicate that non-promotion is common in first grade, and that this non-promotion is chiefly the result of failure in reading.

Studies of first grade reading reveal that failure is even more prevalent in the development of the various specific skills which constitute general reading ability. Typical of these studies is Dolch's [21] comparison of the efficiency of primers in teaching word recognition. He gave a test composed of words in the reading vocabulary of the children to the first grade classes in twelve schools. Out of thirty-one words, the class averages ranged from twenty-eight to eighteen words correctly recognized. If we may take the median class average as representative, the children he tested had failed to learn to the point of recognition 20 per cent of the words selected from their basic vocabulary. The average of the best class was failure to recognize 10 per cent of these words; the average of the poorest class was failure to recognize 43 per cent. It is apparent that, in this one phase of reading at least, children vary widely in their degree of success. Contrasted with the more successful children in most of the classes were others who had developed practically no word recognition. After a year of teaching, they could not recognize even the word "mother."

Needlessness of Many of These Failures

There are many reports of potential reading failures whose failure was prevented by the adjustment of instruction to their needs and

[17] *Survey of the Pasadena City Schools.* 1931.

[18] *Report of the Survey of the Schools of Chicago, Illinois. Summary of Findings and Recommendations.* 1932.

[19] Alabama Department of Education, *Survey of Conecuh County Schools.* 1932.

[20] "Report of the Survey of the Schools of Evansville, Indiana." Unpublished manuscript, 1935.

[21] Edward W. Dolch, "The Efficiency of Primers in Teaching Word Recognition," *Journal of Educational Research*, 28:271–275, December, 1934.

interests. There are also many reports of successful remedial teaching of children who had already failed. Such reports strongly suggest the possibility that many of the failures that occur are unnecessary. In the present study a potential failure is defined as a child who is more likely to fail than to succeed unless some factor or factors of instruction become more favorable.

Some potential failures succeeded because the instruction happened to be of a type that was adjusted to their needs. Both Bond [22] and Fendrick [23] present examples of this. They found that in classes where reading was taught phonetically there was a larger percentage of children with auditory and speech defects among the poor readers than of children with visual defects. Under a look-say system of teaching, there were more children with visual defects among the poor readers than children with auditory and speech defects. Apparently children whose physical limitations would have caused them to fail under one system of teaching succeeded when the instruction happened to be adjusted to their specific needs.

A striking example of the influence of circumstances of instruction on success or failure is reported in a study by Gates and Bond.[24] Two first grade children, who were identical twins, had practically equivalent mental ages, slight hearing and visual defects, and a foreign home background. One was seated in the front of the room near the teacher, the other far from the teacher near a window which opened on a noisy street. The first twin succeeded as well as could be expected of a child with her mental ability. The other was a poor reader. The failing twin, however, rapidly improved in her reading when given individual instruction adjusted to her defects of vision and hearing.

Other potential failures succeeded because the instruction was consciously adjusted to their limitations. Two examples of this type of adjustment in reading instruction are Thompson's work with deaf children and Dunklin's with children of low I. Q. Thompson [25] adjusted the reading to the limitations of the deaf children by using a purely visual approach consisting of many silent reading situations

---

[22] G. L. Bond, *The Auditory and Speech Characteristics of Poor Readers.* 1935.
[23] P. Fendrick, *Visual Characteristics of Poor Readers.* 1935.
[24] A. I. Gates and G. L. Bond, "Reading Readiness; A Study of Factors Determining Success and Failure in Beginning Reading," *Teachers College Record,* 37:679–685, 1936.
[25] Helen Thompson, *An Experimental Study of the Beginning Reading of Deaf Mutes.* 1927.

which did not depend upon use of speech or hearing. At the end of the first year, their silent reading ability was much better than that of the other deaf children. In fact, it was almost as good as the reading of normal children. Dunklin [26] taught a group of low I. Q. children who were unable to read preprimers. He divided the regular reading program into smaller units and supplied for each unit many supplementary reading experiences to insure reading comprehension and mastery of the skills involved in each unit before taking up the next. At the end of the school year, these pupils took all the silent and oral reading tests given in the various first grades of the school. The results of these tests showed that this group of low I. Q. children had learned to read as well as the average first grade class.

The results of remedial teaching give evidence of the needlessness of reading failure in many cases. There is a large, rapidly growing literature which reports how children who had failed were later successfully taught to read. As early as 1922 monographs on the subject were published by both Gates [27] and Gray.[28] The Psychological Clinic [29] of the University of Pennsylvania has published a series of case studies and reports. A general conclusion which may be drawn from these and other reports is that children who have previously failed become successful in learning to read when their instruction is adjusted to their needs and interests.

Some of the earliest articles on remedial teaching were written by Fernald and Keller.[30] They reported in 1921 the successful teaching of non-readers by the kinesthetic method. In the beginning the pupil traced with his first two fingers the outline of a word he wanted to learn, saying the word as he did so. After he was sure he knew the word, he wrote it without looking at the copy, saying the syllables to himself as he wrote them. After learning to associate words with their printed forms, the pupils read from books. Whenever they

[26] Howard T. Dunklin, "How a Group of Reading Failures Was Taught to Read." Unpublished manuscript, 1934.

[27] A. I. Gates, *The Psychology of Reading and Spelling with Special Reference to Disability.* 1922.

[28] William S. Gray, with the cooperation of Delia Kibbe, Laura Lucas, and Lawrence W. Miller, *Remedial Cases in Reading; Their Diagnosis and Treatment.* 1922

[29] Arthur Phillips, "The Clinical Examination and Diagnostic Teaching of Cases at the Psychological Clinic of the University of Pennsylvania," *Psychological Clinic,* 19:169–200, November, 1930.

[30] Grace M. Fernald and Helen Keller, "The Effect of Kinaesthetic Factors in the Development of Word Recognition in the Case of Non-Readers," *Journal of Educational Research,* 4:355–377, December, 1921.

needed to learn a new word or to recall an old one which they had failed to recognize, the full procedure was repeated. In a more recent publication [31] Fernald and Keller report continued success with this method. In fact, once started, their pupils learned even more rapidly than the average child who had experienced no difficulty. Among their cases were adults as well as school children. They consider that their objective for any child has been reached when he is able to participate successfully in the work of his grade. With older children and adults they attempt to develop a higher speed of reading, and to encourage extensive reading to fill in backgrounds which are inadequate.

In 1927, Gates published the first systematic manual for diagnosing and treating reading disabilities.[32] Through competent and careful research over a period of years he has constantly added to the body of information about diagnostic and remedial methods, much of which is embodied in a revision of this book published in 1935.[33] His study of the way children learn to read when they make normal progress has provided standards of attainment and suggestions of method for his remedial cases. His research has included studies of cases handicapped by various factors. However, only a relatively small proportion of his remedial cases have been reported. These are scattered throughout his publications and are usually given briefly as illustrations.

Gates' general method of determining degree of disability is to compare the level of reading ability as indicated by reading tests of various types with the potential learning ability as shown by appropriate mental tests. The child's particular abilities and needs are discovered through the use of diagnostic tests of various types of comprehension and through the inventory type of diagnostic tests which aid in the analysis of various abilities which make up a reader's word recognition techniques. Any abnormal situation with regard to emotional, physical, and background factors is taken into account in the diagnosis and plan for remedial teaching. His teaching method stresses the visual approach. The correction of faulty techniques and the development of adequate reading habits are provided for in reading situations rather than in periods of drill.

[31] Grace M. Fernald and Helen Keller, *On Certain Language Disabilities— Their Nature and Treatment.* 1936.

[32] Arthur I. Gates, *The Improvement of Reading: A Program of Diagnostic and Remedial Methods.* 1927.

[33] *Ibid.* Revised Edition. 1935.

Through word selection and other exercises in context, the child develops these needed techniques in a reading situation.

In 1932 Marion Monroe [34] presented a well analyzed report of the work in remedial reading done under her direction. Her general procedure was to determine the child's initial status with relation to reading by means of a composite of tests of various types of reading. She determined the child's degree of disability and set up objectives for his instruction by comparing his level of achievement on these reading tests with his potential learning ability as indicated by tests of his intelligence and by tests of achievement in other school subjects. Diagnostic tests were used to show the nature of his difficulty. A definite plan of teaching was made for each child, taking into account his special abilities and disabilities. The lessons were so planned that the child was able to attain a high degree of success. His feeling of success was depended upon for motivation.

Monroe's method employed the auditory approach, which seeks to develop ability to discriminate between sounds, and then proceeds by tracing and sounding to develop mastery of increasingly difficult phonetic elements. Great care was taken to find books which were suited to the child's level of ability and interests. Although the mechanics of word recognition were stressed comprehension was kept as the chief goal of reading. During the reading, comprehension was checked constantly. While most of the teaching was done individually Monroe reports successful teaching of small groups of children who had similar needs and about the same level of development.

Recently other diagnostic and remedial programs have appeared but these illustrations indicate the general type of attack, which usually consists of a search for special strengths and weaknesses and for materials and methods of adjusting instruction to them.

Further illustrations describe remedial programs organized according to the same general principles and carried out in public school systems. The success of remedial teaching when materials and methods are adjusted to the child's abilities and needs is strikingly illustrated by the New York City Remedial Reading Project begun in January, 1934 as Civil Works Administration Project Number 69. Bennett [35] reports that in this project more than ten

[34] M. Monroe, *op. cit.*
[35] Annette Bennett, "Launching a Reading Project," Part I, *Journal of Exceptional Children,* 5:82–86, January, 1939.

thousand children who were New York City's outstanding failures in ·reading in the lower elementary grades made an improvement from one and one-half to six times as great as the rate of progress in an average class in an equivalent length of time. Unemployed teachers without special training for remedial reading did the teaching under the direction of twenty-four graduate students of Teachers College and a central organization headed by Dr. Annette Bennett. Each teacher, with some assistance from the supervisor, made her own diagnoses and remedial plans. The teaching was done individually at first, later in small groups of children having like difficulties and similar abilities. The greatest reading difficulty was found to be the limited meaning and reading vocabularies of the children.

The central office prepared "vocabulary units" of reading material, each designed to teach as new words twenty different words from the Gates Primary Word List. A preliminary test for each unit showed the teachers what each child's vocabulary needs were in relation to this unit. Ten to fifteen pieces of reading material were contained in each unit to supply as much practice as the slowest learners needed. The materials were varied in character and so arranged that the child could score his own responses. With this material, teachers were able to work with ten children at a time, helping individuals when necessary while each of the other children worked at his own rate on material best suited to his needs.

Another type of remedial work carried on in public schools is reported by Dunklin.[36] During the school year 1934–35 she worked with the outstanding reading disability cases of various public schools of Buffalo, New York, for brief periods of from two to three weeks, dividing each day between two schools. The general plan of the work was to make individual diagnoses and to give to those children having the greatest need the remedial instruction necessary to overcome the undesirable reading habits which were preventing their progress in reading. When the children had overcome their undesirable reading habits to a degree which enabled them to read successfully at their own level of ability, materials were provided at gradually increasing levels of difficulty. As much as possible of this work was done during the remedial lessons. A diagnosis and plan for further work was given to the regular teacher. In many cases the teacher was able to do little more than assist the child in securing

[36] Laura Dunklin, *Summary of the Report on Remedial Reading for the Year 1934–35*, Department of Education, Buffalo, New York.

the books he needed to read. A few teachers carried on individual lessons of five to twenty minutes a day for varying periods after the remedial teacher had left the school. The remedial teacher maintained contact with the children through weekly letters in the form of blanks to be filled out stating what special reading had been done, and through brief visits at intervals of about two months. The remedial teacher gave demonstrations of individual remedial lessons and of remedial teaching with classroom groups. Through observation of these demonstration lessons by regular teachers a contact was made between remedial and regular teaching. At the end of the school year, retests were given on various phases of reading ability—silent reading, oral reading, and word pronunciation. The average progress made by the children taught individually, according to the results on standardized tests, was twice that expected of average children—two months in one. This progress was 8.9 times what might have been expected of the children had they progressed at the same rate as before the reading instruction.

A description [37] of the remedial teaching carried on by Dunklin with one group of seventeen second grade children having first grade reading ability is particularly applicable to the present problem because of its similarity to the regular classroom situation. These children had been in the first and second grades from two to five years. A diagnosis of reading habits was made in individual interviews supplemented by observation during instruction. Group remedial lessons given for one week stressed the development of each child's awareness of his own needs. Each child was given means of working toward the correction of his undesirable habits. The classroom teacher observed these lessons and carried on the work for the remainder of the semester. Retests of the children in the group mentioned above showed a gain of 10.2 months in five months—slightly more than twice that expected of average children.

With increased school success came an improvement in personality and social adjustment. The classroom teacher of the group described above stated in her report to the remedial teacher: "One of the most satisfactory results is that the children have gained a feeling of security. They read more readily and seem to be happy while doing it. The group on the whole has changed from a slow, uninterested group, to a happy, lively crowd of real workers."

[37] Laura Dunklin, *Special Methods in Reading Class at School No.—*, Board of Education, Buffalo, New York, 1936.

DEVELOPMENT OF A TENTATIVE PROGRAM OF ADJUSTMENT

Essential Qualities of an Adjusted Program

Analysis of the illustrations given shows certain qualities to be essential in the adjustment of reading instruction to the learners' needs. First, the instruction is characterized by an appreciation of individual problems. Second, definite objectives guide the instruction. Third, the child's status with relation to his attainment of these objectives is known at the beginning. Fourth, it is known continuously throughout the course of instruction. Fifth, provision is made for the child's constitutional and other limitations. Sixth, the progress of instruction is adjusted to the child's ability. Seventh, at each step sufficient reading experience is provided to insure success. Eighth, special reading activities are provided with guidance by the teacher to meet specific needs. Ninth, the instruction engages the child's interest and effort. Finally, the adjustment is evidenced by daily success.

In setting up in a regular classroom situation a tentative program of adjusted instruction which will have to an appreciable degree the essential qualities described, certain limitations of the regular classroom situation must be recognized and met. The teaching will be done by average teachers without special training, except that which comes through participation in the program of adjustment. No more than the usual amount of time càn be expected for teaching reading or for preparation of lessons and materials. Classes will be of average size. Techniques of discovering and providing for individual constitutional and other limitations will be restricted to those available through regular school channels. Only materials of instruction which are available in the schools will be used. These restrictions will permit adoption of only *some* of the means used in successful remedial programs. However, most of these means will have to be adapted for use in regular classrooms and in many cases it will be necessary to find substitutes. Each of the essential qualities will be considered and means of attaining them under the above limitations will be sought.

Contributions of Selected Studies to the Tentative Program

Certain studies having direct bearing on the present problem will be considered for the suggestions they offer toward the development of means for attaining the qualities of adjustment under the limitations of the regular classroom.

The instruction is characterized by an appreciation of individual problems. This implies that the teacher knows each child's needs as they occur and gives him the help necessary to overcome his difficulties. In surveying the field of reading disabilities, Gates[38] observes that the inability of the typical teacher thus to individualize instruction is one of the causes of reading disability.

Bennett[39] reports that, when confronted with the necessity of meeting the needs of individual children, her coaches who had only the training common to regular teachers developed the appreciation of individual problems which is characteristic of remedial teachers. As more pupils were added to each teacher's group, such teaching procedures were used and such materials were provided as would enable the teachers to maintain their individual approach by keeping constantly in touch with each child's status in relation to the goals set for him.

The effectiveness of the use of practice materials with beginning first grade children is reported by Smith.[40] Each child in her group was provided with a series of units of silent reading material with comprehension checks. He worked through these materials at his own rate. After one semester the experimental children read as well as the average child usually reads after one year.

Other means of maintaining the individual approach suggested by the various types of remedial teaching described previously include the determination of the child's initial status and the grouping of pupils according to initial status and special needs. Determination of initial status will be considered in detail later. Monroe[41] organized small groups of children having approximately the same level of reading ability and reading needs. Dunklin[42] reports that each child in her second grade group, through consciousness of his own special needs, was able to work toward the correction of his own difficulties while being taught in a classroom group.

[38] A. I. Gates, "Viewpoints Underlying the Study of Reading Disability," *Elementary English Review*, 12:85 ff., April, 1935.

[39] Bennett, *op. cit.*

[40] Nila B. Smith, "An Experiment to Determine the Effectiveness of Practice Tests in Teaching Beginning Reading," *Journal of Educational Research*, 7:213–228, March, 1923.

[41] M. Monroe, *op. cit.*

[42] L. Dunklin, *Special Methods in Reading Class at School No.—*, Board of Education, Buffalo, New York, 1936.

The evidence of these studies indicates that regular teachers can and will, develop an individual approach to remedial teaching when the conditions of teaching encourage it. To encourage this attitude provision probably should be made for some sort of grouping according to reading abilities and an adequate supply of material which is both diagnostic and instructional.

Definite objectives guide the instruction. The methods and materials of the regular program in reading have been formulated on the basis of definite objectives. A statement of these aims was given in the *Twenty-fourth Yearbook* [43] of the National Society for the Study of Education and has been revised and extended in the *Thirty-sixth Yearbook.* [44] Smith [45] states that, following the publication of the *Twenty-fourth Yearbook,* courses of study and basal textbooks have almost universally accepted these objectives and planned their methods and materials to attain them. Cooper [46] found, in her analysis of primers and manuals of reading systems published after the *Yearbook,* that basically they harmonize with its recommendations.

In the examples of adjusted instruction described above, the children who were given remedial teaching were selected because of their serious failure to meet the objectives of regular instruction. The reading diagnosis which preceded remedial instruction contained a definite statement of the child's status in relation to the objectives of reading. The remedial teaching was planned to provide activities which would develop the child's reading ability with respect to these objectives. Accordingly, to set up a program of adjusted instruction in the regular classroom would involve merely an extension of, or a more definite statement of, the objectives already accepted.

The child's status with relation to the objectives of reading is known at the beginning of reading instruction. In the program of adjusted instruction for beginners in reading initial status refers to the child's readiness to begin reading activities, as well as to the types of reading activities best suited to his present state of development. Among the phases of a child's development which previous investigators have considered important for reading readiness are

[43] National Committee on Reading, *The Twenty-fourth Yearbook* of the National Society for the Study of Education, Part I. 1925.
[44] National Committee on Reading, *The Thirty-sixth Yearbook* of the National Society for the Study of Education, Part I. 1937.
[45] Nila B. Smith, *American Reading Instruction,* pp. 190 ff. 1934.
[46] I. M. Cooper, "Comparative Study of the Organization for the Teaching of Ten Beginning Reading Systems," *Journal of Educational Research,* 28:347–357, January, 1935.

mental maturity, previous experience, interest in reading, and physiological maturity.

The mental maturity necessary for beginning reading has been studied from two angles, general mental maturity and specific abilities which are related to learning to read. Many studies dealing with the relationship of mental age to success in learning to read have been published. In 1931 Morphett and Washburne [47] reported a study in which the proportions of children who were successful readers increased for each mental age level up to 6 years and 6 months, remaining constant for higher levels. Success, in this study, signified success in learning to read by means of the Winnetka material.

In the Los Angeles Schools, according to Woods,[48] mental age of at least 6 years and 4 months, with other conditions favorable, was necessary for success in beginning reading. She found that children with a mental age of 6 years and 9 months were practically certain to succeed.

Gates [49] reports for four groups the necessary mental age for success in beginning reading. One of the groups, supervised by Raguse, was provided with a large amount of easy teach-and-test materials to supplement the basic materials. In this group, a mental age of 5 years and o months was satisfactory for success, since there were only 7 per cent who failed to reach a reading grade score of 1.95 at the mental age of 5 years and o months or above. In another group taught in a New York City school by somewhat superior regular teachers using experimental material provided by Gates and his colleagues, a mental age of 5 years and 6 months was satisfactory for success. In a third group, taught by superior teachers with a good supply of regular reading materials but with no specially prepared materials, a mental age of 6 years and o months was satisfactory. In a fourth group, taught in large classes by somewhat inferior teachers with an inadequate supply of reading materials and little provision for individual work, a mental age of from 6 years and 6 months to 7 years was reported as necessary for even a moderate assurance of success.

Judging from the reports of Washburne, Woods, and Gates, the

[47] M. V. Morphett and C. Washburne, "When Should Children Begin to Read?" *Elementary School Journal,* 31:496–503, March, 1931.

[48] E. I. Woods, "A Study of the Entering B1 Children in the Los Angeles City Schools," *Journal of Educational Research,* 21:9–19, September, 1937.

[49] A. I. Gates, "The Necessary Mental Age for Beginning Reading," *Elementary School Journal,* 37:497–508, March, 1937.

necessary mental level for beginning reading depends upon the type of reading program as well as upon the mental age. The question to be considered in the prevention of failure is whether to adjust the reading program to the child's present mental level or to postpone reading until his mental level reaches the "critical mental age" for the program in use. For the child's best general development as well as to avoid possible failure it may seem advisable to postpone formal reading instruction in some cases.

The advantages of postponement stated by different authors are varied. Woods,[50] reporting favorably on the practice of placing immature children (those having a mental age below 6 years and 4 months) in a Transition 1B class to reduce failures, suggests that for normal children as well it might be better to postpone reading instruction until their mental maturity has reached the level represented by average pupils in the second half of first grade (a mental age of 6 years and 9 months). Thomson [51] found that children having mental ages of 6 years or over before systematic reading began progressed more rapidly and enjoyed reading more than children of lower mental ages. Gates and Russell [52] describe the effects of delaying beginning reading a half year with children having I. Q.'s of 75 to 95 and average mental ages of 5 years and 7½ months. They found a small but definite superiority on the part of the children whose reading instruction was delayed for a half year. They offer the opinion that it is better for such children to have a varied and enriched program without reading for the first half year, perhaps longer.

While Gates and Russell believe that the non-reading program was better for this group, they state that a study of individuals who did not succeed revealed problems which needed individual treatment and which would not be solved by mere delay. Their study does not suggest that delay is best for all children.

Mental age scores do not predict reading success with sufficient accuracy to justify their use as the sole criterion for excluding first grade children from reading instruction. Morphett and Washburne [53]

---

[50] E. I. Woods, *op. cit.*

[51] J. L. Thomson, "Big Gains from Postponed Reading," *Journal of Education,* 117:445–446, October, 1934.

[52] A. I. Gates and D. Russell, "The Effects of Delaying Beginning Reading a Half Year in the Case of Underprivileged Pupils with I. Q.'s 75–95," *Journal of Educational Research,* 32:321–328, January, 1939.

[53] M. V. Morphett and C. Washburne, *op. cit.*

report correlations between mental ages as of September, 1928 and measures of reading success in February, 1929, for first grade children; between number of sight words known and Binet mental ages, .58; and between number of progress steps completed and Binet mental ages, .51. The corresponding correlations for mental ages on the Detroit First Grade Intelligence Test were .65 and .59. Grant [54] found a correlation of .63 between mental age on the Pintner-Cunningham Primary Mental Test at the beginning of first grade and reading achievement as measured by a group of standard tests at the end of second grade. Deputy [55] reports a correlation of .70 between the Pintner-Cunningham mental age and a composite score on three reading tests in first grade. Monroe [56] reports a correlation of .57 for the Detroit Intelligence Test with measures of success in first grade reading. Even the highest of these correlations, that reported by Deputy, has a forecasting efficiency of only 29 per cent.[57] The mental age may indicate which children will achieve the greatest success in reading and which will be the least successful. The relative success of the large percentage of children between these extremes will not be predicted by their mental ages. Judged by their mental ages alone, many children would be excluded from reading who could succeed.

Certain specific abilities, as well as the general mental level, have been found to bear a close relationship to success in learning to read. To measure these specific abilities, reading readiness tests have been developed. Smith [58] found that, in general, children who could match letters best during the first week of school were the ones who made the best scores on vocabulary tests at the end of twelve weeks. Ability in matching has been used by the Lee-Clark [59] and other reading readiness tests to select children who are ready for reading. Monroe [60] uses measures of several abilities, such as motor coordination, language development, and visual and auditory memory, and

[54] A. Grant, "A Comparison of the Metropolitan Readiness Tests and the Pintner-Cunningham Primary Mental Test," *Elementary School Journal*, 38:118–126, October, 1937.

[55] E. C. Deputy, *Predicting First Grade Reading Achievement*. 1930.

[56] M. Monroe, "Reading Aptitude Tests for the Prediction of Success and Failure in Beginning Reading," *Education*, 56:7–14, September, 1935.

[57] C. L. Hull, *Aptitude Testing*. 1928.

[58] Nila B. Smith, "Matching Ability as a Factor in First Grade Reading," *Journal of Educational Psychology*. 19:560–571, November, 1928.

[59] J. M. Lee and W. W. Clark, *Reading Readiness Tests*. 1931.

[60] M. Monroe, *op. cit.*

discrimination. The Van Wagenen [61] and the Metropolitan [62] Reading Readiness Tests also include tests of various abilities.

The predictive value of reading readiness tests for success in reading is slightly higher than that of intelligence tests. Deputy,[63] by adding tests of association, comprehension, recall, and word selection, raised the correlation from .70 on the Pintner-Cunningham alone to .75 on the battery of tests. Monroe,[64] who found a correlation of .57 with reading success for the Detroit alone, likewise found a correlation of .75 for a battery of tests. Grant [65] found a correlation of .64 between the Metropolitan Reading Readiness Test given in September, 1935 and a battery of reading tests given in May, 1937. Tests of limited functions give correlations with reading achievement which are lower than those of batteries of tests. An investigation carried on in Buffalo [66] showed correlations of the Lee-Clark Reading Readiness Test with Gates Primary Reading Grade Scores of .25 for Polish, .44 for American, .16 for Italian, and .57 for Negro populated schools. The predictive value for a correlation of .75, the highest reported here, is a little over one-third.[67] Many children who could succeed would be excluded from reading if their scores on reading readiness tests were the sole criterion of exclusion.

A comprehensive discussion of reading readiness was presented by Harrison [68] in 1936. She collected the results of extensive research, formulated a philosophy of readiness for reading, and offered an analysis of the factors in its development. She gave full descriptions of available tests of readiness and explained instructional procedures for developing a state of readiness.

Since the publication of Harrison's book three extensive investigations have given an empirical evaluation of reading readiness tests. Nearly two hundred devices, including practically all those techniques which have been suggested for predicting reading readiness, were used not only with beginners but also with children in all the primary grades. In many cases the same tests or equivalent forms

[61] M. J. Van Wagenen, *Reading Readiness Tests.* 1932.
[62] G. Hildreth and N. L. Griffiths, *Metropolitan Readiness Tests.* 1933.
[63] E. C. Deputy, *op. cit.*
[64] M. Monroe, *op. cit.*
[65] A. Grant, *op. cit.*
[66] Research Committee, "The Prediction Value of the Lee-Clark Reading Readiness Test as Used in the Buffalo Public Schools." *Yearbook of the Buffalo Elementary School Principals Association,* 1937.
[67] C. L. Hull, *op. cit.*
[68] M. L. Harrison, *Reading Readiness.* 1936.

were repeated at intervals during the children's first two or three years of school. Results of these tests were correlated with tests of reading progress. In one investigation, reported in a series of studies by Wilson, Flemming, and their associates,[69] the children were above average in intelligence and background, and were taught in small groups at Horace Mann School. In another investigation, reported by Gates, Bond, and Russell,[70] the children were mainly of average or inferior intelligence, with inferior social and economic backgrounds, and were taught in the large classes of a New York City public school. In a third study, Gates [71] reports the use of a battery of tests (which had proved of highest predictive value in the two previous investigations) with the entire first grade population of a small Connecticut city. The results of these studies indicate that the most effective measures of reading readiness are tests of abilities which will be used in reading, and that their predictive value is proportionate to the degree of their use. For example, tests of letter naming had a high predictive value for children who used letter naming as a word recognition technique in learning to read. These same tests had a much lower predictive value for children who used other techniques for word recognition.

The need for provision of a rich background of experiences in kindergarten as a factor in readiness for reading is described by Hilliard and Troxell [72] in their comparison of the success in reading of two first grade groups, the one with a rich, the other with a meager background. Waters [73] describes how she carried out in her kindergarten a plan for providing the background which would be needed by her pupils in first grade reading. Gard [74] reports that children in grades three, four, and five with kindergarten experience surpassed non-kindergarten children in those same grades in ten of eleven measures of silent reading ability.

[69] F. Wilson, C. Flemming, A. Burke, and C. Garrison, "Reading Progress in Kindergarten and Primary Grades," *Elementary School Journal*, 38:442–449, February, 1938.

[70] A. I. Gates, G. Bond, and D. Russell, *Methods of Determining Reading Readiness*. 1939.

[71] A. I. Gates, "An Experimental Evaluation of Reading Readiness Tests," *Elementary School Journal*, 39:497–508, March, 1939.

[72] G. J. Hilliard and E. Troxell, "Informational Background as a Factor in Reading Readiness and Reading Progress," *Elementary School Journal*, 38:255–263, December, 1937.

[73] D. Waters, "Prereading Experience," *Education*, 44:308, January, 1934.

[74] W. L. Gard, "The Influence of the Kindergarten on Achievement in Reading," *Educational Research Bulletin*, 3:135–138, April, 1924.

Children's personality traits as well as their background of information and skills are affected by their previous experiences. Studies such as Ladd's [75] show the importance of personality traits for success in reading. Habits of work, ability to get along with other people, cheerfulness, persistence, industry, self-confidence, feelings of inferiority, fear of the unknown, desire for attention, overdependence, and other such attitudes may have been established long before school entrance.[76] One problem of the school is the substitution of desirable habits and attitudes for undesirable ones. Another [77] is the adjustment of the school program to the abilities and interests of the child to the end that undesirable habits and attitudes may not be set up in the child by his experiences in school, and that desirable ones may be encouraged.

Interest in books and reading was considered an indication of readiness for reading by one hundred eighty-nine of the two hundred eighty-eight successful teachers whose opinions were reported in a bulletin of the National Education Association.[78]

Physiological maturity is an important factor in readiness for reading. Perhaps the reasons why it has not been studied so extensively as its importance for learning to read would warrant are that: (1) many phases of physiological maturity have reached a level of development beyond that required for learning to read long before the usual age of beginning instruction and (2) other phases of physiological maturity form the bases for functions which are so largely the result of mental activity or environmental influences that they have been studied as mental or environmental rather than as physiological functions. Speech, and handedness are among these phases. Such delays or defects in the development of some phase of physiological growth as handicap the learning of a child otherwise ready to read are considered in another section of this chapter under "Constitutional and Other Limitations."

Betts [79] suggests vision as one phase of physiological development in which children in first grade may be too immature for beginning to learn to read. He points out that the distance between the pupils

[75] M. Ladd, *op. cit.*
[76] C. Bühler, "The Social Behavior of the Child," *Handbook of Child Psychology.* 1931.
[77] Marion Monroe, *Children Who Cannot Read,* pp. 102–105. 1932.
[78] Research Division of the National Education Association, "Better Reading Instruction," *Research Bulletin,* Vol. 13, November, 1935.
[79] E. A. Betts, *The Prevention and Correction of Reading Difficulty,* pp. 66 ff. 1936.

of their eyes is shorter than the corresponding distances of older persons. He also suggests that the child's eyeball, being shorter than that of the mature eye and accordingly farsighted, is not ready for the close work involved in the reading of books.

The child's status with relation to the objectives of reading is known continuously throughout the course of reading instruction. The essential feature of adjusted instruction is that adaptation to individual needs is continuous throughout the course of instruction. The illustrations given show that this continuous adaptation is possible when the teacher has ways of knowing what the child's needs are at every point. Some of the means of diagnosis and of adjustment described in these illustrations can be used in regular classroom instruction, others cannot. For example, oral reading as a means of diagnosis cannot be used as extensively in the average class as in remedial instruction. To the extent that it can be used, however, it can reveal pupils' needs to the regular teacher who has the diagnostic point of view.

To provide reading situations which expose the needs of each pupil or afford opportunities to meet these needs, group silent reading exercises offer a more effective means than oral reading. Bennett [80] in the New York City Project provided such material for use with groups. Smith [81] reports the effectiveness of one type of such materials. Gates' [82] method involves the use of materials which develop word discrimination and other skills in natural reading situations. These teaching materials, being objective, readily show the child's needs. They should be useful in a program of adjustment as means of diagnosis and as means of providing needed reading experiences. Dunklin [83] found that the regular reading materials could be used for such diagnostic and instructional purposes.

Diagnostic programs such as those of Monroe,[84] Durrell,[85] Gray,[86] Gates,[87] Betts,[88] and others provide analyses of the reading process which may show the teacher or experimenter what basic abilities and

---

[80] A. Bennett, *op. cit.*

[81] N. Smith, *op. cit.*

[82] A. I. Gates, *New Methods in Primary Reading.* 1928.

[83] L. Dunklin, *Special Methods in the Reading Class at School No. —,* Board of Education, Buffalo, New York, 1936.

[84] Marion Monroe, *Children Who Cannot Read,* pp. 183–201. 1932.

[85] D. D. Durrell, *Durrell Analysis of Reading Difficulty.* 1937.

[86] W. S. Gray, *Remedial Cases in Reading: Their Diagnosis and Treatment.* 1922.

[87] A. I. Gates, *The Improvement of Reading,* pp. 503–628. 1935.

[88] E. A. Betts, *op. cit.,* pp. 311–383.

needs to look for. Suggestions for the preparation of diagnostic materials may be evolved from some of these programs, especially those which include group tests. Several of their procedures for individual testing may be adapted for use with groups.

Provision is made for the child's constitutional and other limitations. A necessary feature of adjusted instruction is that it discovers those constitutional and other limitations of each child which might interfere with learning to read, and takes them into account in the instruction. Studies of children who have already failed indicate which of these limitations most often accompany reading disability. Hooper [89] found that of 145 repeaters in first and second grades 41 had no physical defect, 20 had enlarged tonsils, 19 showed malnutrition, 14 had hearing defects, and 12 had visual defects. Of 94 of these failures, 69 per cent had Binet I. Q.'s below 90. Eames [90] compared the physical handicaps shown by reading disability cases with those shown by a group of unselected children. The disability group showed much larger percentages of visual defect. The differences in general physical condition slightly favored the unselected group. Many other limitations are more potent than physical defects in causing reading failure. After reviewing the causative factors of reading defect, Monroe [91] concludes that reading defect is due to the operation of a group of factors rather than to any one factor. Gates [92] and Durrell [93] believe that much failure is the result of faulty reading habits caused by the inadequacy of instruction or equipment. In providing for the limitations of low intelligence, Gates,[94] basing his recommendation on the results of previous investigations, suggests that in comparison with normal children these children of low intelligence are interested [95] in the same material, but that they need more of it. Such provision for low I. Q. children as Gates [96] describes was

[89] L. Hooper, "What about School Failures?" *Elementary School Journal,* 36: 349–353, January, 1936.

[90] T. H. Eames, "A Frequency Study of Physical Handicaps in Reading Disability and Unselected Groups," *Journal of Educational Research,* 29:1–5, September, 1935.

[91] Marion Monroe, *Children Who Cannot Read,* p. 110, 1932.

[92] A. I. Gates, "Viewpoints Underlying the Study of Reading Disability," *Elementary English Review,* 12:86–90, April, 1935.

[93] D. D. Durrell, "Tests and Corrective Procedures for Reading Disabilities," *Elementary English Review,* 12:91–95, April, 1935.

[94] A. I. Gates, *Interest and Ability in Reading,* p. 35. 1930.

[95] M. B. Huber, *The Influence of Intelligence upon Children's Reading Interests.* 1928.

[96] A. I. Gates, *The Improvement of Reading,* pp. 403–410. 1935.

found to be successful with Dunklin's [97] group of low I. Q. children.

Three general classes of visual defect have received notice in the literature: errors of refraction, imbalance of the exterior eye muscles, and unequal images or aniseikonia. Betts [98] offers a technique for discovering visual defects which might be corrected by an eye specialist. Eames [99] describes how a non-reader with a severe eye-muscle incoordination was taught to read by the use of large type material. Fendrick's [100] results suggest that children with visual difficulties have a better chance of success under a phonetic method of teaching than under a look-say method. However, .the results of other research [101] suggest that most beginners in first grade are not sufficiently mature to make a profitable use of phonics.

Children with hearing and speech defects have a much greater chance for success when taught by a look-say method than when taught by a phonetic method.[102] The deaf mutes studied by Thompson [103] learned to read successfully by the exclusive use of silent reading materials.

Certain children have normal hearing but do not have a normal ability to discriminate sounds. Other children may have normal vision but lack normal visual discrimination. For those children who have poor auditory discrimination, Gates [104] suggests that phonics be tried, but given up if the method is unsuccessful. For those with poor visual discrimination exercises to develop sharp perception of words are recommended.

Delayed maturation of some phases of physiological growth may give rise to constitutional limitations. While most children begin to show a definite preference for the right or left hand during the first year of life [105] and by the age of five show much greater skill in the use of the preferred hand,[106] some children come to first grade with-

[97] H. Dunklin, *op. cit.*, p. 37.

[98] E. A. Betts, *op. cit.*

[99] T. H. Eames and R. W. Peabody, "A Non-Reader Reads," *Journal of Educational Research*, 28:450–455, February, 1935.

[100] P. Fendrick, *op. cit.*

[101] E. W. Dolch and M. Bloomster, "Phonic Readiness," *Elementary School Journal*, 38:201–205, November, 1937.

[102] G. L. Bond, *op. cit.*

[103] H. Thompson, *op. cit.*

[104] A. I. Gates, *Improvement of Reading*, pp. 429 f. 1935.

[105] H. S. Lippman, "Certain Behavior Responses in Early Infancy," *Journal of Genetic Psychology*, 34:424–440, September, 1927.

[106] B. Wellman, "The Development of Motor Coordination in Young Children," *University of Iowa Studies: Studies in Child Welfare*, 3:93, 1926.

out having established hand dominance. Likewise, by the age of three years more than 75 per cent consistently prefer one eye.[107] By the age of five or six years, most children have become definitely right- or left-eyed. The child who enters first grade without having established laterality or one whose dominant eye and dominant hand are on opposite sides is considered by Orton [108] as one who has failed to establish unilateral cerebral dominance. He believes that, unless these children have a special type of teaching, they will develop a type of reading disability which he calls strephosymbolia. Stanger and Donahue [109] describe methods of discovering and teaching these children to prevent reading disability. Their method of teaching is painstakingly slow and laborious. Exponents [110] of other methods report as great success with this type of child as with other children.

Among the incorrect responses made by beginners in reading, reversals have received a great deal of attention. Teegarten [111] finds a correlation between scores on her test for reversal tendency before reading instruction began and reading achievement at the end of the first grade, of .54 for children with kindergarten experience and .77 for children who had not attended kindergarten. Orton [112] considers reversals an indication that the child has failed to establish unilateral cerebral dominance. Gates and Bennett [113] report that they found no one type of eyedness or handedness to be consistently associated with a reversal tendency in reading. They describe both preventive and remedial instruction. Hildreth [114] found that as children progress through the grades, their number of reversals decreases. Apparently for most children the incidence of reversals is an indication that the left to right directional habit in reading has not yet been completely established.

The tentative program of adjustment should provide several types of material, some emphasizing one means of learning, some another.

[107] R. Updegraff, "Ocular Dominance in Young Children," *Journal of Experimental Psychology,* 15:758–766, 1932.

[108] S. T. Orton, "Specific Reading Disability—Strephosymbolia," Journal of the *American Medical Association,* 90:1095–1099, April 7, 1928.

[109] M. Stanger and E. Donahue, *Prediction and Prevention of Reading Difficulties.* 1937.

[110] G. Fernald and H. Keller, *op. cit.*

[111] L. Teegarten, "Tests for the Tendency to Reversal in Reading," *Journal of Educational Research,* 27:81–97, October, 1933.

[112] S. T. Orton, *op. cit.*

[113] A. I. Gates and C. C. Bennett, *Reversal Tendencies in Reading.* 1933.

[114] G. Hildreth, "Reversals in Reading and Writing," *Journal of Educational Psychology.* 24:1–20, January, 1934.

In this way it will be able to meet the needs of children having various constitutional limitations. It will be possible to use the same kinds of material for several types of limitations. For example, a greater than usual supply of reading material at each level is recommended for children of low intelligence, for those with foreign background, and for those having hearing defect.

The progress of instruction is adjusted to the child's ability. The final success of pupils in adjusted instruction is dependent upon success in each step of the program. As the teacher is constantly aware of the pupils' needs, she shapes the instruction to progress by steps within their ability. A group of first grade children described by Stone [115] affords an excellent example of the need for this type of progression of reading materials. After a half year's instruction by a good teacher these pupils were described as non-readers. The group began all over again, using easier material. All these children made satisfactory progress during the remainder of the semester.

The attempt to read too difficult material may break down good reading habits and encourage the formation of inadequate habits, as is graphically shown by photographs of eye movements made by Judd and Buswell.[116]

The choice of basic reading materials within the children's ability is an important factor in the adjustment of instruction. This is illustrated by the work with the first grade class described by Stone.[117] De Long [118] describes the classification of reading materials and the organization of reading instruction in the primary grades according to Stone's Reading Levels. In many measures of reading ability at the end of first grade Gates and others [119] report that a group of children taught by a modern systematic method using a planned sequence of materials surpassed a group taught by an opportunistic method.

The amount of supplementary material needed will depend upon the limitations of the children and the adequacy with which the basic

[115] C. Stone, *Better Primary Reading*, pp. 7–9. 1936.

[116] C. H. Judd and G. T. Buswell, "Silent Reading: A Study of the Various Types," *Supplementary Educational Monographs*, No. 23, University of Chicago, November, 1922.

[117] C. Stone, *op. cit.*

[118] V. R. De Long, "Primary Promotion by Reading Levels," *Elementary School Journal*, 38:663–671, May, 1938.

[119] A. I. Gates, M. I. Batchelder, and J. Betzner, "A Modern Systematic versus an Opportunistic Method of Teaching: An Experimental Study." *Teachers College Record*, 27:679–700, April, 1926.

instruction provides for the children's progression by steps within their ability. In selecting or constructing this supplementary material, it is necessary to avoid introducing new difficulties. For example, Gross [120] and Rudisill [121] find that some preprimers and primers differ widely in their vocabularies from other preprimers and primers. Care should be taken to select as supplementary material books with a vocabulary sufficiently like that of the basic material to introduce few new words.

At each step, sufficient reading experience is provided to insure success. A major factor in Thompson's [122] success in teaching reading to deaf mutes, and of Dunklin's [123] success with children of low I. Q. was the provision of as many reading experiences at each level as were necessary for mastery of the difficulties of that level. Provision was made by Bennett [124] for supplying her remedial teachers with sufficient material to give each child the reading experiences he needed.

A plentiful supply of material is here understood as material within the child's ability. Material which is too difficult, however plentiful, is without value. While a child is reading one preprimer he may, because of difficulty in vocabulary,[125] find a preprimer of another series too difficult. Later, when he has reached a higher level of ability, he may read the second preprimer with profit.

Special reading activities are provided with guidance by the teacher to meet specific needs. Guidance in the development of desirable reading habits and skills may be accomplished by the use of work type or other materials and by direct instruction on the part of the teacher. Monroe,[126] for example, developed sound discrimination by using series of pictures of objects, the names of which contained the sounds to be recognized or discriminated. Gates [127] shows how various techniques of word recognition may be developed in the silent reading of work type materials. This use of such materials, which he

[120] A. Gross, "A Preprimer Vocabulary Study," *Elementary School Journal,* 35: 48–56, September, 1934.
[121] M. Rudisill, "Selection of Preprimers and Primers—A Vocabulary Analysis." *Elementary School Journal,* 38:683–693, 767–775, May and June, 1938.
[122] H. Thompson, *op. cit.*
[123] H. Dunklin, *op. cit.*
[124] A. Bennett, *op. cit.*
[125] M. Rudisill, *op. cit.*
[126] Marion Monroe, *Children Who Cannot Read: The Analysis of Reading Disabilities and the Use of Diagnostic Tests in the Instruction of Retarded Readers.* 1932.
[127] A. I. Gates, *New Methods in Primary Reading.* 1928.

describes as the intrinsic method, also provides practice in the use of context clues while developing various types of comprehension.

The effectiveness of silent reading material in the development of specific skills is greatly increased when the child is conscious of the aim and striving to attain the skill for which he is practicing. Gates reports that a remedial case taught by means of intrinsic materials and with teacher guidance made an improvement greater than that of a child taught by means of intrinsic materials alone. Dunklin,[128] in teaching the group of remedial cases described above, found that each child, through a consciousness of and an attempt to correct his own undesirable word recognition habits, was able to do so while all were working on the same intrinsic materials.

The instruction engages the child's interest and effort. This quality is the concern of reading programs in general as well as of the program of adjustment. Basic methods and materials of reading instruction, as was mentioned previously, have been affected by scientific studies of children's reading and interests and the statement of objectives in the *Twenty-fourth Yearbook.*[129] The tentative program of adjustment will work in harmony with the basic program, since it is based on regular methods and materials which are interesting to the children.

The program of adjustment has an additional contribution to make to the children's interest in reading, in that it provides for their greater success in learning. The kindergarten children in Meek's [130] experiment on the learning of words began the "game" with a high degree of interest, which was maintained by those who succeeded. The unsuccessful children, however, after several experiences of failure, developed a strong distaste for the activity.

The adjustment is evidenced by daily success. Day by day success was the aim of the programs from which the essential qualities of adjustment have been derived. Similarly the extent to which the tentative program is able to attain the foregoing qualities will be manifested by the degree to which it is successful day by day.

The Tentative Program of Adjustment

A consideration of means available for attaining the essential qualities of adjusted instruction under the limitations of facilities

[128] L. Dunklin, *Special Methods in the Reading Class at School No. —*, Board of Education, Buffalo, New York, 1936.
[129] National Committee on Reading, *op. cit.*
[130] L. H. Meek, *Study of Learning and Retention in Young Children.* 1925.

available in the regular classroom suggests the following plan.

1. Regular teachers will be used. These teachers may need some assistance in assimilating the philosophy of adjustment. They may need to develop techniques of using the reading materials which will enable them to be constantly aware of pupils' needs which they must meet. The means used to aid the teachers in acquiring these new points of view and techniques may include bulletins, lectures, or talks with the person directing the adjustment.

2. The program of adjustment will use the regular materials supplemented by published or specially prepared materials. These additional materials required for adjustment of instruction will exceed little, if at all, the amount ordinarily allowed for supplementary use. They will depend for their results upon their specific teaching value and their diagnostic character. A plan for a prohibitive amount of materials might make the program of adjustment impossible in a regular school situation.

3. The program will be carried on in classes of average size. To facilitate adjustment of the instruction, groups of children having similar needs will be formed within the class. At first the groups will be formed according to the methods ordinarily used by the school. Later the diagnostic material of the adjusted program will guide the shifting of pupils from one group to another.

4. No more than the usual amount of time will be spent by the class in reading or by the teacher in planning and preparing materials. This will be the case when the person directing the instruction selects and supplies the material or when a group of teachers cooperatively work out such a program. Should a teacher plan to carry on the program independently, she would necessarily spend more time in preparation.

STATEMENT OF THE PROBLEM

A survey of the literature of primary reading has resulted in the formulation of the tentative program of adjusted instruction described in the preceding pages. This tentative program will be used experimentally to determine what degree of success may follow its application.

The problem of this experiment is: Can reading failures in first grade be prevented to an appreciable degree by such adjusted instruction as is possible in a city school system?

CHAPTER II

PROCEDURE

ORGANIZATION OF GROUPS FOR THE EXPERIMENT

THE matched group technique was used in this experiment. Control and experimental groups were formed in each of three public schools in the city of Buffalo, New York. Subjects were chosen from among those children who, in November, 1935, seemed most likely to be failures in reading at the end of their first grade.

Choice of Schools

Schools were chosen whose first grade population offered a sufficient number of potential failures to justify an experimental group and a control group of at least fifteen members each. The Director of Primary Grades helped in the selection of schools by making available the statistics covering the first grade population and percentage of failures in the preceding year for each school in the system.

The Buffalo schools have a large first grade population coming from non-English-speaking homes. Since this factor is commonly regarded as one of the causes of failure to learn to read in first grade, it was considered in the selection of the schools.

On the basis of language background, size of school, and percentage of failure in the preceding year, Schools A, B, and C were chosen. School A is a primary school with a first grade enrollment in September, 1935 of 198 children predominantly from Italian-speaking homes in one of the poorest sections of the city. The children are sent to kindergarten as young as the school will admit them. The percentage of first grade failure in School A for the year 1934–35 was 52. School B is a primary annex with an assistant principal in charge. It had a first grade enrollment in September, 1935 of 100 children predominantly from Polish-speaking homes in an average residential section of the city. A majority of the children enter first grade without kindergarten experience. The percentage of first grade failure in School B for the year 1934–35 was 20. School C is an eight-grade school with a first grade enrollment in September, 1935 of 90 children predominantly from English-speaking homes, many of them Jewish. The school is in one of the better residential sections. Practically all of the first grade children in this school had attended kindergarten. In the first grade of School C the percentage of failure for the year 1934–35 was 15.

Teachers of the Experimental Groups

In each school, the experiment was discussed with the principal. A teacher for the experimental group was tentatively chosen. This teacher was given a description of the experiment, including the duties and privileges it would involve for her, and she was allowed to choose whether or not she would participate.

The teachers were representative of teachers in the system as a whole. All were normal school graduates who had taken several extension courses since graduation. By this means one teacher had earned a Bachelor of Science degree in Education. All had had more than five years' experience in primary education in Buffalo. According to rating on teaching ability by their respective principals the group was representative of the total group of teachers in the city.

Selection of the Children

For the purposes of this study, it was necessary to have an objective and uniform measure to discover the potential failures in reading. The selection of the children for the experiment was made during the tenth week of school. At that time most of the classes had completed the preparatory period of instruction and were about to begin the reading of books. By waiting until this stage in the instruction it was possible to measure directly the children's ability to learn to read, instead of measuring it indirectly by means of intelligence or reading readiness tests. The classes differed so widely in the amount and selection of their reading material that it would have been difficult, if not impossible, to predict their future degree of success by measuring their accomplishment on material already taught.

A learning-to-read test seemed to offer the most adequate measure for predicting reading success. The use of such a test is in accordance with McCall's[1] fundamental principle for equating groups: that they must be equal in their capacity for growth in the experi-

[1] William A. McCall, *How to Experiment in Education*, p. 41. 1923.

mental trait. The lesson was taught and the test given by the same unfamiliar teacher-examiner with a uniform procedure to every first grade class in the three schools. Each first grade teacher submitted a vocabulary list of the material she had taught. The learning-to-read lesson and test was so constructed as to use none of these words. Thus each child had an equal opportunity to show his ability to learn new material.

The material and method of application of this lesson-test were developed in cooperation with the teacher-examiner who was to give it. This teacher was a normal school graduate who had had experience in teaching in kindergarten. Because of her accuracy in carrying out the details necessary from the research point of view and because of her skill in handling the children, she was chosen to do all further testing for the experiment.

The lesson was presented in a uniform manner to each class. The teacher brought in a white mouse. She talked with the children about the mouse, bringing out in the discussion certain words and phrases which were to be met in the reading material. The mouse was put away "to sleep," and each child was given a four page booklet, each page of which had a sentence about the mouse with an illustrative picture. After the booklets had been read, the four sentences were reread from charts emphasizing the phrases which most aptly described the four pictures of the booklet.

Each child was given a practice sheet which contained two exercises. In the first, the sentences of the booklet were printed in sequence opposite miniature reproductions of the pictures in a different order. The children were to draw lines from these pictures to the appropriate sentences. In the second exercise, phrases were used in place of complete sentences. The teacher-examiner taught the children the method to be used by means of a chart which was a facsimile of the exercise, and gave further practice in reading the sentences and phrases. As the children did the work of the practice exercise she gave assistance where necessary and made certain that every child had learned the technique.

One hour after this lesson, she returned and, without assisting the children further, gave the learning-to-read test, the results of which were to be used in selecting the children for the experiment. This test consisted of a copy of the practice exercise described above and two more sheets of similar material, having in all twenty-two items. The working time of this test was about twenty-five minutes.

The coefficient of reliability of the learning-to-read test was .88. This was derived by use of Spearman's formula [2] from a correlation of .79 ± .012 between odd and even items for 388 cases of low first grade children.

The validity of the test as a means of finding potential failures was indicated by its correlations with other means used for this purpose and by its correlation with measures of success at the end of the experiment. For 317 first grade children the test had a correlation of .59 ± .02 with teachers' estimates expressed on a five-point scale, and with scores on the Lee-Clark Reading Readiness Test [3] a correlation of .707 ± .02. This latter correlation became .765 when corrected for attenuation with a formula suggested [4] by Spearman. For the control group of fifty-four children, the average correlation coefficient of the learning-to-read test with the Gates Primary Reading Tests I, II, and III and the Gates Oral given seven months later was .46. This correlation between the test lesson and a measure of achievement at the end of the experiment for children who were selected for their low scores on the test would be equivalent [5] to a correlation of 88 for the entire 317 first grade children. This agrees with the usual practice of indicating validity by correlation coefficients based upon the entire range of normal groups.

Formation of Groups for the Experiment

Experimental and control groups were formed in each school from among those children who showed the poorest ability in the learning-to-read test described. The relationship of scores of experimental and control groups to the scores of the general first grade population in their schools is shown in Table I.

[2] $r_x = \dfrac{2r_h}{1 + r_h}$. H. E. Garrett, *Statistics in Psychology and Education*, p. 271. 1926.

[3] J. M. Lee and W. W. Clark, *Reading Readiness Test Manual*. 1931.

[4] $r_{AB} = \dfrac{r_{A1B1}}{\sqrt{r_{A1A2} r_{B1B2}}}$. See Garrett, *op. cit.*, p. 213.

[5] Using the formula (derived from Kelley's formula 25), $\dfrac{\sigma}{\Sigma} = \dfrac{\sqrt{1 - R}}{\sqrt{1 - r}}$

$R = 1 - \dfrac{\sigma^2}{\Sigma^2}(1 - r)$, in which R is the correlation coefficient derived from distributions with a standard deviation of Σ, and r is the correlation coefficient derived from distributions with a standard deviation of σ. T. L. Kelley and E. Shen, "General Statistical Principles," *The Foundations of Experimental Psychology*, p. 849. 1929.

TABLE I

AVERAGE SCORES OF TOTAL, EXPERIMENTAL, AND CONTROL GROUPS
ON THE LEARNING-TO-READ TEST

Group	School A			School B			School C			Total		
	N	Ave.	S.D.	N	Ave.	S.D.	N	Ave.	S.D.	N	Ave.	S.D.
Total First Grade Population	151	12.14	6.29	89	15.36	5.90	77	16.82	5.46	317	14.18	6.33
Experimental	28	7.93	2.25	14	10.29	3.16	12	10.58	3.78	54	9.13	3.16
Control	28	7.50	2.02	14	10.14	3.05	12	10.75	3.03	54	8.91	2.94

Table I gives average scores of the total group in each school on the learning-to-read test as well as scores for those children who remained in the control and experimental groups at the completion of the experiment. In the beginning, there were 60 children each in the control and experimental groups, but only 54 in each group took part throughout the experiment.

School A had a sufficiently large first grade population and percentage of potential failures to justify the formation of experimental and control groups of thirty each. At Schools B and C half class units of fifteen children each were formed. Accordingly, the experimental teachers of Schools B and C each taught as the other section of her class a group superior in learning ability to the experimental pupils. In each school, the experimental group was taught by one teacher. The control children were left scattered among the other first grade classes. To avoid changes in their instruction because they were in the control group, their identity was not announced during the progress of the experiment.

To keep the experimental and control groups as nearly homogeneous as possible, experimental and control groups were drawn from the population of potential failures in the same schools. The proportion of boys to girls in the experimental and control groups was arranged to be the same as that of the entire first grade population of their school. Children who had been in first grade before were excluded from the experiment.

Table II shows that there was no statistically reliable difference between the experimental and control groups in regard to the criteria upon which they were matched.

TABLE II

TABLE II

MATCHING CRITERIA FOR CONTROL AND EXPERIMENTAL GROUPS

Group	Scores on Learning-to-Read Test		Age in Months		Sex	
	Ave.	S.D.	Ave.	S.D.	Boys	Girls
Experimental............... N 54	9.13	3.16	75.70	4.32	24	30
Control.................... N 54	8.91	2.94	75.15	4.98	24	30
$\dfrac{D}{S.\,D.\,\text{diff.}}$ *	.37		.68			

* As there is no correlation between members of the experimental and control groups, the formula
$$\sigma_{\text{(diff)}} = \sqrt{\sigma^2_{\text{(av.1)}} + \sigma^2_{\text{(av.2)}}}$$
is used for this table. See Garrett, *op. cit.*, p. 129.

THE ADJUSTMENT OF INSTRUCTION

The foundation of adjusted instruction is the clear understanding of the needs of each pupil, not only at the beginning but continuously throughout the entire course of his instruction. The effectiveness of adjusted instruction depends upon the degree to which this understanding guides the provision of adequate materials and methods.

Materials of Instruction

Basic materials. The Gates-Huber first grade materials [6]—textbooks, workbooks, and teachers' manual—were chosen as the basic materials of instruction. Since they were already available in the school system and have a general plan in harmony with that of the experiment, these materials, when supplemented as needed, afforded a good foundation for the adjusted instruction.

Supplementary materials. The supplementary materials written for the experiment were provided in a variety of forms. The general purposes were to determine which children needed more practice for mastery of the materials and to supply appropriate reading experiences as their needs were shown. These further reading activities were so planned as to present the necessary experience in a setting of

[6] Arthur I. Gates and M. B. Huber, *The Work-Play Books,* Primer, Preparatory Book, and First Grade Manual. 1930.

material already mastered. In this way the learner's attention was
directed toward accomplishing the aim set for him. Practically all
of these activities were presented in reading situations. Most of them
were in the form of original stories with such aims as increasing
fluency and giving greater familiarity with the vocabulary while
maintaining a high degree of interest. Others were planned to develop habits of accurate word perception within sentences or to
correct incipient habits of inaccurate word perception. The material
was so arranged that each child's mastery was clearly indicated by
the responses he made. Comprehension of the reading material was
constantly fostered and checked by these exercises.

At the end of each unit of work, a diagnostic test was given which
measured: (*a*) mastery of the vocabulary, (*b*) use of this vocabulary
in comprehension of new material, (*c*) number of ideas within one
sentence each child could read and illustrate, (*d*) techniques of
word recognition, and, after the introduction of letter sounds, (*e*)
ability to identify spoken sounds within printed words.

Independent reading materials. These materials were of three
types—the set of thirty-six books supplied each class by the public
library, published books selected for the purposes of the experiment,
and specially constructed books with illustrations gathered from
various sources and with original text hand-lettered in India Ink.
The public library books were too difficult for independent reading
by the children. The published books selected for the experiment,
though easier reading than the public library books, were not so
widely chosen by the children for reading as were the specially constructed books, which carried the burden of the program for free
reading. Carefully graded in difficulty, these books offered reading
material easy enough for any level of ability found among these
children.

The books for independent reading were always easier than the
level of difficulty the groups had reached in their basic materials.
They were short enough to permit complete reading at one sitting.
Comprehension tests were supplied for the early materials.

Instruction

Reading instruction. The general plan of instruction followed the
manual of the Gates-Huber material. This was modified in accordance with the results of research surveyed in Chapter I. To attain
the aims of adjusted instruction, techniques for diagnosis and teach-

ing were adapted or evolved. According to the plan the child was so prepared by previous reading activities that he read each story in the Gates-Huber Reader with ease and pleasure. First, he read silently and completed individually the preparatory materials in the workbook. During the silent reading the teacher gave him whatever guidance seemed necessary. Group oral reading and discussion of the preparatory materials just completed led to each child's scoring of his own responses. It was possible for each child to know at once just what his difficulties were and to replace with the correct response any tendency to error. Children who needed further practice were given the appropriate supplementary material, while those who did not need extra practice were allowed to enjoy free reading or to engage in other activities which the teacher had planned.

When ready, the class read the story in the Reader silently first with guidance as needed, then orally. While the story usually was read in one lesson period, the preparatory activities might require several lesson periods. Meanwhile the related activities and conversation or oral English periods were providing further experience and background information.

There was no provision in the plan for class word drills or extensive oral development of reading materials. However, there was provision for each child to receive an adequate preparation by means of reading experiences adjusted to his needs.

Independent reading. The books for independent reading were first read silently when other work was completed or during library periods. As with the other reading materials, children were encouraged to take them home to read to others. In some cases they were permitted to read these books to other first grade classes. Whenever a child felt that he was ready, he did the comprehension exercise for the book. Later in the year the children were encouraged to select and read parts of the more difficult books from the public library. The children of one of the classes became interested in forming their own personal libraries of booklets that had been mimeographed as preparatory material.

Writing, spelling, and phonics. The teaching of writing, spelling, and phonics in the experimental groups was combined into one activity as a part of the experiment. The words learned and the skills formed in writing, spelling, and phonics are closely related to the word recognition techniques used in reading. It seemed to the experimenter to be essential, therefore, that consistent rather than conflicting techniques for word learning be developed during all these phases of word study. In Schools A and B, the children used cursive writing; in School C, manuscript. The visual method of teaching spelling was adapted to give more emphasis to phonetic analysis of the words learned. The early lessons were worked out in detail, since the teachers had never used this method before. The words taught were selected with the following criteria in mind: inclusion in the Horn-Ashbaugh First Grade List [7] (required by the School Department); degree of ease in writing and spelling; graded introduction of new letters; usefulness in developing phonetic ability; order of occurrence in reading vocabulary; and usefulness in writing sentences. All this work was postponed until the second semester.

Instruction of non-experimental groups. In Schools B and C, the experimental groups comprised only half the class. The instruction of the other half of the class, composed of children of greater ability than either the control or the experimental group, was outside the province of the experiment. In School B, however, the experimental teacher requested that she be supplied with the experimental material to enable her to follow the same plan of instruction with her non-experimental group. School C followed an activity program. The reading instruction of this non-experimental group was very different from that of the experimental group. However, this teacher adopted the experimental plans for spelling, writing, and phonics for use with her non-experimental group.

Means Used in the Development of Teacher Participation

The degree of effectiveness of the adjusted instruction as planned in this experiment was dependent upon the teachers' cooperation, their adoption of the purposes of the adjusted instruction, and their development of skill in using the means provided.

To develop this teacher participation, the experiment used group meetings, general letters on method and interpretation of pupil responses, teacher reports, and visits to schools. The teachers met at intervals of about six weeks at the home of the experimenter to discuss general problems that were arising. Among these problems, the most important seemed to be conflicts between the methods of teaching they had been using and those suggested for the experiment. The problems of individual children were brought up for con-

[7] E. Horn and E. Ashbaugh, *Progress in Spelling, Grades One to Four.* 1935.

sideration and suggestions made for further materials or changes in instruction.

General letters were sent out to introduce each new type of material. In other letters an attempt was made to clarify points on which there seemed to be some confusion. Following receipt of the reports on the diagnostic tests, specific suggestions were sent out for improving techniques of word recognition for those children who showed poor techniques. The teachers were urged to report weekly, or more often if some need arose. (The experimenter left stamped, self-addressed envelopes for their use.) . For this purpose mimeographed lists of their pupils' names were supplied to use in noting each child's difficulty as it occurred. It was hoped that this analysis of individual difficulties would help the teacher to become more definitely aware of individual needs, and more able in making the necessary adjustment.

Had it been possible to visit the classes during reading lessons, the adjustment would have been much easier for both the experimenter and the teachers. Visits to the schools were made before or after school to organize the experiment, to leave materials, and to confer with individual teachers.

Intelligence Tests

Intelligence tests were given to the children of the experimental group. The Pintner-Cunningham Primary Mental Test [8] was given in November and the Otis Primary [9] in June by the same teacher-examiner who had given the learning-to-read tests. Most of the experimental children were also given the Stanford Revision of the Binet Test [10] by a certified school psychologist.

Physical Examination

Three physicians of the Buffalo Health Department gave a physical examination covering those defects which were considered [11] most likely to handicap progress in learning to read. In the examination of the eyes, binocular and monocular acuity, both distant and near, was tested. Astigmatism, muscle imbalance, and other defective

[8] R. Pintner and B. Cunningham, *The Pintner-Cunningham Primary Mental Test*. 1928.
[9] A. Otis, *Otis Group Intelligence Scale, Primary Examination: Form A.* 1920.
[10] L. H. Terman, *The Measurement of Intelligence.* 1916.
[11] G. L. Bond, *The Auditory and Speech Characteristics of Poor Readers*, 1935; also P. Fendrick, *Visual Characteristics of Poor Readers*, 1935.

conditions of the eye were investigated. The ears were tested separately for acuity in the pitch range of the human voice. Unhealthy conditions of the ears such as sores, scabs, and excessive wax were also noted. To check on the general health, an examination was made of the heart, lungs, tonsils, adenoids, teeth, and state of general nutrition.

A more detailed description of the methods and materials used will be found in the Appendix, "Adjusted Instruction as Used in This Experiment."

INSTRUCTION OF THE CONTROL GROUPS

In order that the comparison of the control and experimental groups at the close of the experiment should give a valid measure of the effect of the adjusted instruction, it was necessary that the instruction of the control groups resemble as closely as possible the instruction that ordinarily would have been given the experimental children if they had not participated in the experiment. The control children, had they been known to their teachers, might have been given instruction they would not otherwise have received. In order to reduce the probability of such additional instruction, the experiment left the control children anonymous during the experiment. To insure instruction representative of their schools, the control children were left scattered among the other first grade classes.

In the initial investigation each of these children received exactly the same amount of attention that was given to every other child in the first grade classes of Schools A, B, and C. In preparing for the experiment the attention was focused upon the members of the experimental groups. Any shifts which were made of children from one class to another were obviously to secure well balanced experimental groups, although they also helped to secure well balanced control groups. Until the time for final measurement of progress, only the experimenter knew the names of the children in the control groups.

The control children were given the same instruction as the other children in their schools. In School A, the first grade classes used the Gates-Huber Reader and workbook as basic materials. The teachers were familiar with the method of teaching described in the manual for these materials, having used it for some time. As supplementary reading materials, the teachers composed and used many work-type reading exercises on the blackboard or in mimeographed form. They also used books from the general school supply which were available to the experimental groups. They had sets of books from the public library similar to those available in the experimental classes.

The situation in School B was similar to that in School A with regard to supplementary materials and library books. However, some of the classes used the Gates-Huber materials as basic materials, while others used the Elson-Gray series.

School C differed from the other schools in providing reading instruction of an activity type in which no basal reader was used. In other respects, their supply of materials was equal to or perhaps more plentiful than that in Schools A and B. In addition to the books from the public library, the children had classroom libraries made up of their own books which they were encouraged to lend to their classmates.

MEASURES OF SUCCESS

During the seventh month of the experiment, tests were given to measure the accomplishments of the experimental groups, the control groups, and the non-experimental groups taught with the experimental classes in Schools B and C. All these tests were given by the same teacher-examiner who had given the learning-to-read test for the selection of the experimental and control pupils at the beginning of the experiment.

Silent reading ability was tested with the Gates Silent Reading Tests, Primary, Types I, II, and III.[12] The Gates Oral Context Test [13] was used to test oral reading ability and the Gates written spelling of ten standard words [14] to test ability in spelling. These tests were administered according to the directions in the manuals wherein they are described.

A second learning-to-read test was given. This test was constructed according to the plan followed for the first one. The reading material contained seven words believed to be unfamiliar to all the children in a setting of words common to the primers used by both experimental and control groups. Following the reading lesson they were tested on their knowledge of the unfamiliar words. The reliability coefficient of this test was .98 derived by use of Spear-

[12] A. I. Gates, *Gates Primary Reading Tests, Manual.* 1935.
[13] A. I. Gates, *The Improvement of Reading*, pp. 533–539, 606–608. 1935.
[14] *Ibid.*, pp. 565, 624.

man's formula [15] from a correlation of .96 ± .005 between odd and even items for 152 cases of first grade children.

As a further measure of accomplishment, records were secured of school marks, promotion, and attendance.

SUMMARY OF PROCEDURE

1. On the basis of language background, size of school, and the percentage of failure in the first grade for the preceding year, Schools A, B, and C were chosen for the organization of experimental and control groups. The members of these groups were selected from the lowest third in each school as rated on a learning-to-read test given in a uniform manner to all the first grade pupils of these schools. The learning-to-read test was planned as a means of locating the potential failures. The experimental and control groups were matched for their scores on this test, for age, for sex, and for previous school experience.

2. A program of instruction for the experimental children was planned, using a set of basic reading materials supplemented by original materials to reveal and to meet individual needs as they developed.

3. The instruction of the children in the control groups was, so far as possible, left unchanged by the experiment being conducted in their schools.

4. The effectiveness of the adjusted instruction was measured after seven months by standardized tests, a second learning-to-read test, and school marks for control and experimental groups.

5. The materials and procedures used in this experiment were limited by the plan to those available in the average school system.

[15] H. E. Garrett, *op. cit.*, p. 271.

CHAPTER III

ANALYSIS OF DATA

SUCCESS OF THE PLAN

Average Grade Scores on Standard Tests

THE results on the standardized tests given early in June to the experimental and control groups are shown in Graph I in terms of average grade scores for each group. Since the normal grade score for the final month in Grade I is 1.9, a base line has been drawn in the graph to represent this level.

The average achievement of the experimental group was clearly superior on all tests to that of the control group. In every test, the average of the experimental group was above the normal grade score of 1.9, and in no case below a grade score of 2.0. The average scores of the control group were at least two months below the norm in all tests except oral reading. The average silent reading grade score of the control group was 1.65 or .25 of a grade below the level expected according to the norm. The average silent reading grade score of the experimental group was 2.07 or .17 of a grade above the level expected according to the norm. The average oral reading grade score of the control group was 2.2 or .3 of a grade above the norm, while the same test showed the average grade score of the experimental group to be 2.4 or .5 of a grade above the norm. This superiority of both groups in oral reading seems to indicate that in all these classes, oral reading received a greater proportion of the emphasis than is generally true in educational systems sampled for standardization of the tests. The average spelling grade score of the control group was 1.7 or .2 of a grade below the norm, while that of the experimental group was 2.2 or .3 of a grade above the norm.

Statistics of Raw Scores on Measures of Success

Statistics of the raw scores on the final tests, which are shown in terms of grade scores in Graph I, are presented in Table III with the scores of the final learning-to-read test. The numbers of scores are less than 54 for some tests because a few children were not present.

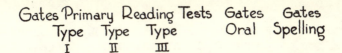

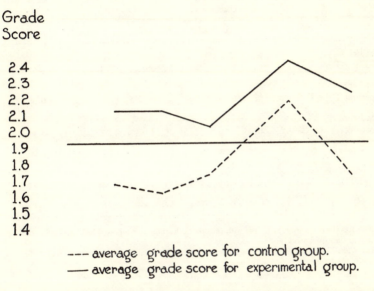

--- average grade score for control group.
—— average grade score for experimental group.

GRAPH I

AVERAGE GRADE SCORES OF EXPERIMENTAL AND CONTROL GROUPS IN THE FINAL
MONTH OF GRADE I ON STANDARD ACHIEVEMENT TESTS

The ratios of the differences between the means of experimental and control groups with the standard deviations of these differences indicate a general superiority of the experimental over the control group on these tests. All of these ratios except that for oral reading are statistically significant, being well over 3, which is considered to indicate practical certainty of a real difference. The ratio for oral reading was 1.86, which indicates that the chances are 96 in 100 that the experimental group has a real superiority in oral reading ability.

While the silent and oral reading and the spelling tests were measures of what had already been learned, the final learning-to-read test was indicative of ability to learn new material. On this test, the experimental group showed a significant superiority over the control group. This seems to indicate that the experimental in-

TABLE III

AVERAGES OF RAW SCORES FOR CONTROL AND EXPERIMENTAL
GROUPS ON FINAL MEASURES OF SUCCESS

Test	Experimental				Control				D **
	N	Ave.	S.D.	$r_{x_1y_1}$*	N	Ave.	S.D.	$r_{x_2y_2}$*	S.D. diff.
Gates Primary Reading Type I....	54	18.70	7.44	.285	54	10.24	8.62	.413	5.87
Gates Primary Reading Type II...	54	23.81	6.67	.173	54	15.04	7.87	.454	6.69
Gates Primary Reading Type III..	53	12.72	3.66	.344	49	6.57	4.57	.499	8.31
Gates Oral..........	53	2.20	2.12	.242	54	1.53	1.81	.489	1.86
Final Learning-to-Read Test........	52	20.98	5.03	.178	54	14.66	6.14	.326	6.02
Gates Spelling.......	53	4.15	1.60	.104	54	2.67	2.16	.409	4.23

* r indicates the correlation coefficient with the original learning-to-read test which was used as the basis for matching the experimental and control groups.

** The Wilks-Lindquist formula for the standard deviation of the difference of means of matched groups was used in the form:

$$\sigma_{M_{y_1} - y_2} = \sqrt{(1 - r^2_{x_1y_1}) \frac{\sigma^2_{y_1}}{N_1} + (1 - r^2_{x_2y_2}) \frac{\sigma^2_{y_2}}{N_2}}$$

The third term has been omitted because there is no correlation between the matched groups. See: S. S. Wilks, "The Standard Error of the Means of 'Matched' Samples," *Journal of Educational Psychology*, 22: 205–208, March, 1931; and E. F. Lindquist, "The Significance of the Difference between 'Matched' Groups," *Journal of Educational Psychology*, 22: 197–204, March, 1931.

struction was successful in one of its chief aims—that of developing in the children techniques by means of which their ability to learn the new vocabulary of reading material was improved.

Comparison of the Number of Failures in Experimental and Control Groups

A comparison of the number of children failing in experimental and control groups may be taken as a measure of the success of the experimental instruction. This comparison can be stated in terms of non-promotion into second grade or in terms of grade scores on standard tests.

Table IV shows the number of children who were not promoted in the experimental and control groups. School A's standard of promotion demanded an unusually high level of achievement for promo-

TABLE IV

NON-PROMOTION OF EXPERIMENTAL AND CONTROL CHILDREN

SCHOOL	NUMBER OF CHILDREN IN EACH GROUP NOT PROMOTED		PERCENTAGE OF CHILDREN IN EACH GROUP NOT PROMOTED	
	Experimental	Control	Experimental	Control
A................	8	27	28.6	96.4
B................	0	5	0	25.7
C................	1	1	8.3	8.3
Total..........	9	33	16.6	61.1

tion. School C stressed other factors of development in its standard of promotion.

The standards of promotion varied so greatly that some children who failed in one school would have been promoted in another. School non-promotion, therefore, offered an unsatisfactory means of comparison for the purposes of the experiment. A more uniform basis was found in the use of an average of each child's grade scores on the three silent reading and the oral reading tests. Since every child could not be expected to reach the norm for the grade, an average reading retardation of more than one and one-half months was arbitrarily chosen to indicate failure. Failures according to this standard are shown in Table V.

TABLE V

NUMBER AND PERCENTAGE OF CHILDREN IN EXPERIMENTAL AND CONTROL GROUPS WHO FAILED TO ATTAIN AN AVERAGE GRADE SCORE OF 1.75

SCHOOL	NUMBER		PERCENTAGE	
	Experimental	Control	Experimental	Control
A................	3	20	10.7	71.4
B................	0	5	0	25.7
C................	3	5	25.0	41.7
Total..........	6	30	11.1	55.5

By either means of determining the number of children failing, the experimental group showed a decided superiority over the control group.

SUCCESS NOT DUE TO FACTORS OTHER THAN THE EXPERIMENTAL INSTRUCTION

The only known factor related to progress in reading in which the experimental group differed from the control group was the factor of the adjusted instruction. Since the groups were drawn from the first grade populations of the same schools, they had the same general environmental influences. The two groups were matched for age, sex, and ability in learning to read new material. The teachers of the control groups were ranked on the average as equal to the teachers of the experimental groups. The similarity of the two groups was assured by the care which was taken in matching them during the organization of the experiment.

TABLE VI

AVERAGES OF NON-EXPERIMENTAL GROUPS ON MEASURES OF SUCCESS IN JUNE

School	Grade Scores					Percentage on Final Learning-to-Read Test
	Gates Type I	Silent Type II	Reading Type III	Gates Oral Reading	Gates Spelling	
B..........	2.43	2.70	2.40	2.90	2.20	99
C..........	2.37	2.15	2.40	2.70	2.70	83

During the progress of the experiment the only change made in the teaching methods of the experimental group was the adjusted instruction. The teachers were not expected to do extra work outside of school time. In the Buffalo Public Schools, the time allotment for reading in the first grade is 400 minutes a week, which allows a twenty minute period every morning and afternoon for each section of a two-section class. One hundred and twenty minutes are allotted each week for phonics and 50 minutes for writing. According to the plan of this experiment, the experimental children were given two reading lessons a day which used no more time than was regularly allotted for reading activities.

Table VI shows that the other groups (non-experimental) who were taught with the experimental groups at Schools B and C were not neglected in favor of the experimental groups in their classes. The average scores of the non-experimental groups on the tests given at the end of the year show a satisfactory achievement.

PRACTICABILITY OF THE PROGRAM OF
ADJUSTED INSTRUCTION

The degree of adjustment of the instruction planned in this experiment required only facilities which would be available in the average school system. The basic materials, textbook, workbook and manual, were already in use in the schools. The mimeographed supplementary material did not exceed the amount which might ordinarily have been made for all three classes. All the teaching was done by regular classroom teachers. The plan for the adjusted instruction required no more time than that usually allotted for reading activities.

In the experiment, available facilities for intelligence tests and physical examinations were used. Group intelligence tests were given by a teacher, individual intelligence tests by a school psychologist. The physical examinations were conducted by school physicians. Significant findings are reported in a later section of this chapter.

CONDITIONS WHICH AFFECTED THE SUCCESS OF
THE ADJUSTED INSTRUCTION

Comparison of Schools

Table VII summarizes the achievement of the experimental group by schools. It shows that the group in School B was consistently the most successful except in the spelling test. School A ranked second and School C third in reading achievement as shown by the average grade score. School C ranked second to School B and above School A in ability to learn to read as measured by the final learning-to-read test. In spelling, School C surpassed both the other schools.

Table VIII presents the average scores of the three schools on the initial learning-to-read test, average initial ages, and average days attended. These data show that the children in School C began with the highest ability to learn to read as measured by the initial learning-to-read test, that School B had almost as high an average score, and that School A was much lower than either of the other two. On age, however, the group in School C ranked third, their average age being 4.21 months less than that of the group in School B, and 1.29 less than the group in School A. In days attended, the group in School C again ranks lowest, their attendance averaging

TABLE VII

SCORES OF SCHOOLS A, B, AND C ON MEASURES OF SUCCESS

Measure	School Average			Total Average
	A	B	C	
Gates Primary Reading Type I Grade Score......	1.95	2.37	1.95	2.1
Gates Primary Reading Type II Grade Score.....	1.95	2.45	1.8	2.1
Gates Primary Reading Type III Grade Score....	1.95	2.3	1.95	2.0
Gates Oral Reading Grade Score............	2.1	2.7	2.1	2.3
Average Reading Grade Score...........	1.99	2.46	1.95	2.13
Gates Spelling Test Grade Score...........	2.0	2.0	2.4	2.2
Final Learning-to-Read Test Score.............	19.27	23.36	21.92	20.98

TABLE VIII

DATA FOR SCHOOLS A, B, AND C ON SOME FACTORS
AFFECTING SUCCESS

Measure	School Average			Total Average
	A	B	C	
Initial Learning-to-Read Test Score....................	7.93	10.29	10.58	9.13
Initial Age in Months.........	75.29	78.21	74.	75.76
Days Attended During School Year 1935–36..............	176.	174.	168.	174.

six days less than that of School B and eight days less than that of School A.

Further conditions affecting success are indicated in Table IX, which lists defects [1] found in the physical examination. Data in this

[1] A report of each child's defects with the suggestions made by the physicians was given to each teacher. She made whatever adjustments were possible in the

table indicate that the children in the group at School C were handicapped to a greater degree by visual defects than the children of either of the other two schools, and that the children of School A were the least handicapped in this respect. In general physical condition, the children of School C appear to be the most handicapped, although the incidence of nutritional defect is greatest in School A.

The general superiority of the group in School B on achievement in reading was accompanied by first rank in age and a middle position in the initial learning-to-read test, days attended, and physical condition. The middle position of the group in School A on reading achievement was accompanied by middle position in age, lowest rank on initial learning-to-read test, and highest rank on days attended and physical condition. The lowest position of the group at School C on reading achievement was accompanied by lowest position in age, highest rank on initial learning-to-read test, and lowest rank in days attended and physical condition.

When consideration is given to the relatively small difference between the groups in Schools A and B as compared with the difference between them and School C on days attended and physical condition, it appears that the degree of success in reading achievement varies with age, days attended, and freedom from physical defects. It seems doubtful, however, that the group in School C was so much younger than the other groups as to be handicapped by the factor of age, especially when this group was able to surpass the others in average score on the initial learning-to-read test.

Poorer attendance and poorer physical condition may explain in part why the superior learning-to-read ability shown by the group in School C failed to result in superior reading achievement. These disadvantages fail to account for the decided superiority of this group on the spelling test, as their influence would naturally have had the opposite effect.

A possible explanation of the superiority of the group in School C in spelling lies in the method of instruction. Both the experimental and the non-experimental groups in School C were taught spelling by the plan for the experimental groups as described in Chapter II. In spelling there was no conflict between the two groups for the teacher's interest and attention. She adopted the new spelling plan

---

classroom and explained to the mother what should be done. Wherever the family could not afford to have the correction made, the school nurse was asked to make the necessary arrangements if possible.

TABLE IX
DEFECTS FOUND BY PHYSICAL EXAMINATION

Defect	School A N = 26		School B N = 12		School C N = 11		Total N = 49	
	Found	Cor-rected*	Found	Cor-rected*	Found	Cor-rected*	Found	Cor-rected*
Eyes								
Acuity-Distant								
O.D.	2				3	2	7	2
O.S.	3		4	1	4	3	11	4
Both								
Acuity-Near								
O.D.								
O.S.	1						1	
Both								
Astigmatism	1				4	2	5	2
Muscle Imbalance			2		1		3	
Other								
Inflammation of Eyelid	6						6	
Ears								
Acuity								
Right								
Left								
Other								
Sores								
Scabs								
Excessive Wax	6		5		10		21	
Heart								
Tachycardia	1		2				3	
Mitral Regurgitation					1		1	
Lungs								
Rales Scattered	1**						1	
Tonsils								
Removed Prior to Examination		3		6		7		16
Defective	5		2		2		9	
Adenoids								
Removed Prior to Examination		3		5		7		15
Defective	5		1				6	
Teeth								
Caries	1		2		6	3	9	3
Nutrition								
Undernourished	2						2	
Glandular Disease								
Enlarged Cervical Gland	9		3				12	

* Corrections had been made prior to examination.   ** This child was convalescing from bronchitis.

and approved of it. Perhaps it was easier for her to assimilate the experimental spelling plan into her teaching because in comparison with the reading plan it was simpler, more definite and supplied with more detailed lesson plans. There was a definite conflict, however, between the method of teaching reading planned for the experimental group and the method which the teacher used by choice with the non-experimental group. The attempt to use both methods and the fact that her background seemed to her to be out of harmony with the experimental method, were hindrances in her assimilation and execution of the experimental reading plan.

Comparison of Experimental Failures with the Total Experimental Group

Conditions which affected the success of the adjusted instruction with individual pupils become apparent when the six children who failed were compared with the total experimental group. Table X summarizes the pertinent information for these failures.

All the failures in the experimental group were rated by their teachers lower than the average of the low group as a whole before the experiment began. While one of the children was very young, four of the six failures were as old as or older than the average age of the experimental group. On the Pintner-Cunningham Primary Mental Test, the mental ages of all of the children who failed were lower than the average, while on the Stanford-Binet, only two were lower than the average. On the initial learning-to-read test, three of the failures were above the average, and three below. Two of the children had no physical defects noted, two had defective vision, one had enlarged cervical glands, and another had defective tonsils and a generally poor physical condition. Four of the children had a lower attendance than the average for the experimental group.

No one factor appears to explain the failure of these six children. Although they had mental ages below the average of the experimental group fifteen of the children who succeeded had mental ages below this average. A similar circumstance existed with regard to the teacher's estimates, twenty-nine successful children having been rated below the average of the experimental group.

Each child who failed showed some inferiority which might explain the failure of the adjusted instruction to reach him. Child 1 showed a general inferiority to the average of the experimental group, as evidenced by mental age on both intelligence tests and

TABLE X

RATING OF EXPERIMENTAL FAILURES AND THE TOTAL EXPERIMENTAL GROUP ON FACTORS WHICH MIGHT HAVE AFFECTED SUCCESS

Child	School	Sex	Teacher's Estimate*	Chronological Age**	Pintner-Cunningham Mental Age**	Stanford-Binet Mental Age**	Initial Learning-to-Read Test	Attendance†	Physical Defects
1...........	A	G	5	6-5	6-1	6-1	7	162	
2...........	A	B	5	6-3	5-11	6-5	10	179	Generally poor condition
3...........	A	B	5	5-6	5-8	5-8	9	175	Enlarged cervical gland
4...........	C	B	5	6-1	5-10	6-8	10	128	Defective vision
5...........	C	G	5	6-2	6-4	6-7	15	126	Defective vision
6...........	C	G	4	6-3	5-2	6-4	4	161	
Average of total experimental group........			3.9	6-2	6-6	6-4	9.13	174	

* Rated before the experiment on a scale of 5, with 5 as the lowest rating.
** Chronological and mental ages as of September, 1935.
† Total days attended during the school year 1935–36.

score on learning-to-read test. Her loss of one and one-half months of school combined with her somewhat inferior mental level may have caused her failure.

Child 2 had a poor general physical condition which may have caused his failure. His Binet score showed he was not inferior to the average in mental level. His Pintner-Cunningham score possibly reflects the tendency of his physical condition to lower his efficiency when not stimulated to do his best by personal contact.

Child 3 was eight months younger chronologically than the average. His mental age on both intelligence tests, though higher than his chronological age, was still below average. He had enlarged cervical glands. Perhaps the conclusion is justifiable that he was too young to succeed with the degree of adjustment provided in his instruction.

Child 4 and Child 5 were each absent three and one-half months during the first semester. This alone might explain their failure. Both had visual defects.

Child 6 was absent about one and one-half months. She was a child with a foreign language handicap in a school of children from English-speaking homes. It was obvious by the responses on her Pintner-Cunningham Test that she lacked sufficient understanding of the English vocabulary to pass some of the sub-tests.

The comparisons of the schools and study of the six failures seem to indicate that the following are the most potent factors in preventing the full success of adjusted instruction in this experiment: poor attendance and uncorrected physical defects. Despite the operation of these factors, from among 54 potential failures in reading the adjusted instruction as applied in this experiment saved 48 from failure, while from a similar group of 54 potential failures the regular school instruction saved 24.

SUMMARY

1. In the final measures of success, the experimental and control pupils attained the following average grade scores on standard tests:

On three Silent Reading Tests, Gates Primary, Type I, Word Recognition; Type II, Sentence Reading; and Type III, Paragraph Reading; the average reading grade score of the experimental group was 2.07, of the control group, 1.65.

On the Gates Oral Context Test, the average grade score of the experimental group was 2.4, of the control group, 2.2.

On the Gates Spelling Test, the average grade score of the experimental group was 2.2, of the control group, 1.7.

The normal grade score for the final month of first grade as expressed in these tests is 1.9. The experimental group meets this standard with all average grade scores at 2.0 or above. The control group fails to meet this standard with all average grade scores, except for oral reading, at 1.7 or below.

2. The superiority of the experimental over the control group in the final tests is indicated by the following critical ratios for the differences of the averages of raw scores:

Gates Primary Reading Tests,	Type I,	5.87
	Type II,	6.69
	Type III,	8.31
Gates Oral Context Test,		1.86
Final Learning-to-Read Test,		6.02
Gates Spelling,		4.23

The ratio for the Gates Oral Context Test indicates that the chances are 96 in 100 that the experimental group has a real superiority in oral reading. The ratios for all the other measures are greater than 3, which is considered to indicate practical certainty of a real difference.

3. Percentages of failure based on school records were 16.6 per cent for the experimental group and 61.1 per cent for the control group. On a more uniform standard, success on standardized tests, 11.1 per cent of the experimental and 55.5 per cent of the control group failed to attain an average grade score of 1.75.

4. The degree of adjustment of the instruction used in this experiment required only facilities which would be available in the average school system.

5. Study of the six experimental pupils who failed to attain an average reading grade score of 1.75 indicates as limiting factors in the success of the adjusted instruction, extended absence from school and uncorrected physical defects.

CHAPTER IV

CONCLUSIONS AND SUGGESTIONS FOR FURTHER STUDY

THE following conclusions can be drawn from the study reported on the preceding pages.

1. Reading failures in first grade can be prevented to an appreciable degree by such adjusted instruction as is possible in a city school system.

2. Through the use of informal diagnostic testing materials, it is possible to discover wrong or inadequate reading techniques in their beginnings, and, by means of guidance and the use of appropriate reading materials, to develop desirable reading techniques.

3. Adjustment of instruction to the needs and abilities of the learners depends upon the teacher's adoption of a diagnostic point of view and upon her proficiency in the use of means for discovering and meeting the individual needs of her pupils.

4. A supply of reading material, either published or especially prepared, which will afford each child successful reading experiences at each stage in his development is a necessary part of the adjustment.

5. Poor attendance and uncorrected physical defects on the part of the pupil limit the effectiveness of adjusted instruction.

6. The first grade child's welfare should be the deciding factor in planning his program. Under some circumstances, a program which enables him to learn to read will be advisable. Under others, one of the many types of non-reading programs will best serve his needs. Further research may show under what circumstances each program is preferable.

PROBLEMS SUGGESTED FOR FURTHER STUDY

Among the issues encountered in the conduct of the present study, six seem most worthy of further investigation.

1. How permanent are the effects of adjustment of reading instruction during the first grade?

  a. Will the superiority in reading ability of the experimental groups over the control groups continue?

  b. Will the experience of success in first grade continue to influence the personality of these children in subsequent years?

2. How effectively could adjusted instruction be used with different types of children, for example, the unstable or the superior?

3. How effectively could adjusted instruction be used with other types of basic reading programs?

4. What more effective means might be used for keeping the teacher of large groups continually informed concerning the needs of her pupils?

5. What effect has ability grouping upon a program of adjusted instruction in first grade reading?

6. Under what conditions is a non-reading program preferable to an adjusted program of reading in first grade?

APPENDIX

ADJUSTED INSTRUCTION AS USED IN THIS EXPERIMENT

THE MEANING OF ADJUSTED INSTRUCTION

Definition

ADJUSTED instruction is instruction so fitted to the child's abilities and needs that he is continuously succeeding and growing. In this experiment, it is understood to mean that part of a complete reading program which so supplements any method of teaching reading as to meet continuously the needs of each individual while it conserves the social and practical values of group teaching. As considered here, it uses only facilities commonly available in the average school.

The complete reading program is a large and important part of the life of the average first grade child. His present success in reading is dependent upon and grows out of the abilities and experiences he brings to this reading program. It, in turn, contributes to his further intellectual, emotional, and social development. It provides opportunities for many types of expression. Under its guidance he acquires certain habits and skills essential to the reading process itself.

Adjusted instruction is an essential part of such a complete program. It supplements the regular reading program to the extent necessary to enable the teacher to fit that program to the abilities and needs of each child. In order to make such an adjustment, she needs to have clearly in mind the objectives of her program, she needs to know continuously each child's level of attainment of these objectives, and she needs to be able to give him the further guidance and practice he may require at each level. To the degree that the regular program of reading does not meet these needs, supplementary materials and techniques should be applied.

Any reading program, with objectives that can be definitely stated, is able to use adjusted instruction advantageously. However, programs differ widely in value. When the success or lack of success of each individual is constantly evident, the poorer programs will be

57

found to need much more supplementation. In some cases they may even require modification to remove features that are found to be conducive to failure.

It is important that the adjustment be a continuous day-by-day process. Whatever the program of reading followed, the growth of some children will not coincide with the increase in difficulty of the reading as planned for their group. At any level of difficulty, some children will need less reading experience than others of their group, and may lose interest or develop undesirable habits if held too long at this level. Some may fail to achieve the current objectives. If the teacher is in constant touch with the progress of each child, she can give him the supplementary guidance or reading he needs in order that the present difficulty will not handicap his future progress.

In the experiment, the advantages of having the instruction continuously adjusted to the needs of each individual were attained without sacrifice of the practical and social advantages of group instruction. Since the teachers kept constantly informed as to the progress of each child, they were able to divide their classes into two or more groups for a part of the reading instruction. Each group was composed of children who, at the time, showed most nearly the same reading needs. Much of the adjustment required was made through these groups. Thus the individual adjustment needed was reduced to an amount that was practical and possible in an average classroom.

Disadvantages of Unadjusted Instruction

When reading instruction is not adjusted to the child's ability to learn, his attitudes, skills, and reading experiences all suffer. Too easy reading may delay the child's progress in acquiring a larger vocabulary and in developing skills in the techniques of reading. Failing to present sufficient challenge, it may cause him to lose interest. Too difficult reading may cause even more serious harm. The child who is confronted in every lesson with many words he has failed to learn will almost certainly lose hope, and become convinced that he is too stupid to learn to read. Such a conviction will interfere with his learning even that material which he would otherwise be able to learn. Since he has little hope of getting the meaning from the printed material itself and has not developed adequate word recognition skills, he guesses wildly from pictures or tries to recall how the passage has been read before by some other child.

When the reading program is considered unmodifiable, and an attempt is made to adjust the child to the reading instead of adjusting the reading to the child, procedures similar to the following are likely to be used. One common procedure is to use much of the reading time in preparatory word drills and other non-reading activities. This practice leaves little time for real reading experience. The little reading done under this plan is likely to be "study" reading, the children working it out word by word as they attempt to apply what they recall from the preparatory drills. This procedure develops habits of slow reading and of thinking in words rather than in larger units.

Another equally undesirable plan of adjusting the children to too difficult reading material is to have them read and reread small portions of the material until they seem to have mastered it. This method encourages memorization of the material rather than the development of desirable reading habits. It greatly restricts the amount of reading done. It wears out the children's interest in reading.

Partially adjusted programs, also, are unsatisfactory. These programs may adjust the reading to meet only one factor, such as the abilities or the interests of the group. Programs which meet only the factor of ability ignore the results of making reading an uninteresting task. At its worst, this type of partially adjusted instruction presents to the reader successions of disconnected sentences whose only purpose is to give each word its due number of repetitions. At its best, such a program offers the child little that he wants to read. This deprives him of an opportunity to develop a love of reading. As a result, the child's development of reading skills is handicapped by lack of motive.

Programs which are concerned only with the factor of interest ignore the dangers of too difficult materials. Even adults, with their superior reading knowledge and skills, do very little reading of scientific articles despite the absorbing interest they experience in reading the material of these same articles when presented by a popular writer in simple language. Children who are given material that is too difficult for them to read tend to satisfy their interest by looking through the books and by listening to others read them. If they try to read material which is beyond their ability, they are likely to develop undesirable habits and unfavorable attitudes toward reading.

Types of Adjustment Required

Three types of adjustment to the reading needs of children are considered here. They are adjustment by non-instructional means, adjustment by the kind of instruction offered, and adjustment by the amount of instruction.

Adjustment by non-instructional means. The handicaps which can be adjusted best by non-instructional means may be classified as physical defects, undesirable personality traits, and harmful environmental influences. Ideally, no child should be put into a situation in which he must try to learn to read while suffering from a remediable handicap which might interfere with his learning to read, or which might be aggravated by the attempt. In the experiment, the children were given a physical examination and an attempt was made to have corrected the remediable defects which were discovered. To assist in this adjustment children with poor hearing and vision were seated near the source of instruction.

The following examples are illustrative of the way individual problems were met. One boy who was color-blind ceased to appear very different from his classmates in the reading work they were doing when he was given a set of crayons labelled with the color names. Another boy with a weak heart was spared the possible strain of the tests required to supply the data on progress. However, his second grade teacher during the following year described him as one of the best readers in her class.

Environmental factors and personality traits which interfered with the children's learning were investigated in home visits or conferences with the parents at school. One child showed indications of a developing attitude of fear toward reading in school. On a home visit it was found that her father had been whipping her to make her learn to read the too difficult library books she had been taking home. Her father seemed glad to learn that her reading ability was more satisfactory than he had feared. He agreed to place less emphasis upon reading at home, and to help her to enjoy whatever reading she did at home by correcting her errors kindly and by praising her successes. This plan was furthered at school by encouraging her to take home only material she could read successfully.

Adjustment by the kind of instruction offered. Some children seem to be able to learn to read as readily by one kind of instruction as another. Other children are so limited in varying degrees by their particular handicaps that they are more likely to respond successfully to certain kinds of teaching in reading than to others. Such handicaps include visual and hearing disabilities, poor sound discrimination and speech defects. The studies of Bond [1] and Fendrick [2] show that children with visual defects are more likely to succeed under a type of instruction that stresses phonetics than under a type that stresses the visual approach. The reverse is reported to be true of children with hearing defects. The adjusted instruction offered by the present experiment provided methods and materials of various kinds to meet such needs. Children who learned little through one kind found others in sufficient variety and amount to enable them to succeed in learning to read.

Adjustment by the amount of instruction offered. Children vary in the amount of reading experience they require at any point in the process of learning to read. The less mature and the less intelligent children and those with meager backgrounds or insufficient use of English will require more reading experience at each level. Some children may require additional instruction only at certain points where they have difficulty. Other children, returning after an absence or entering from another class, need additional instruction before they are able to take part profitably in the reading experiences of their group. This experiment attempted to provide sufficient material to meet these various needs.

MEANS BY WHICH THE TEACHER CAN KEEP HERSELF INFORMED OF HER PUPILS' NEEDS

Before the teacher will be able to adjust her instruction to the needs of any child she must know his present needs. The teachers in the experiment obtained this information to a sufficient degree of accuracy by means of observation of pupil behavior in reading situations, analysis of pupil responses on teaching materials, and analysis of pupil responses on diagnostic tests.

Teacher's Observations of Pupil Behavior in Reading Situations

For the convenience of the teachers in making such notes on observations as they desired for their own use during the experiment, mimeographed sheets were supplied, listing the names of their pupils

---

[1] G. L. Bond, *The Auditory and Speech Characteristics of Poor Readers.* 1935.
[2] P. Fendrick, *Visual Characteristics of Poor Readers,* 1935.

who participated in the experiment. Beside each child's name was a space for notes. The teacher had a sheet at hand during each reading period and noted after any child's name such needs as she observed. These notes were very brief—a suggestive word or abbreviation. Usually notes were made on only a few of the children, since the majority either read satisfactorily or revealed needs which were met during the reading period. The sheets were dated and labelled to identify them in relation to the reading material.

These observations were concerned with general "reading health," inadequacies of skill development, and specific difficulties. The following are some of the more important phases of pupil responses which it was found helpful to observe:

Interest. The teacher needs to be alert to any lack of interest whether it be toward reading itself or toward any particular type of material or topic. She should look for the cause of such lack of interest, and remove it or compensate for it in so far as possible. Frequently a lessening of interest is observed as a result of material which increases in difficulty so rapidly that the child no longer derives satisfaction from reading it.

Emotional attitudes. Attitudes which might handicap progress include fear of failure, a conviction of inferior ability to learn, or worry about reading. Indications of such undesirable attitudes in oral reading are a tense or high-pitched voice, unwillingness to read before the group, or failure to attempt any reading not thoroughly known. In silent reading the child may show uncertainty by frequent attempts to copy or to get help in other ways. One of the advantages of adjusted instruction is the rarity of such unfortunate attitudes. The year after the experiment, several second grade teachers spoke of the outstandingly desirable attitudes of the experimental children in their classes.

Comprehension. Understanding of the material may be determined to some extent by the expressiveness of oral reading. Phrasing or rhythmic reading is an indication of comprehension of these larger units. In either silent or oral reading, comprehension is most clearly indicated by the discussion or the comprehension exercises which follow reading. These will be discussed more fully in a later part of this section.

Expression. A child may understand reading material very well, yet read it in a manner that is not pleasing. Expressive oral reading increases the interest of the listeners as well as that of the reader.

The oral reading period provides an opportunity for noting and correcting deficiencies in enunciation, pronunciation, and voice control.

Word recognition. One of the most common difficulties noted was lack of recognition of specific words which certain children had not learned after some experience with them. Consistent trends in errors in word recognition such as confusions of words similar in form like *here* and *there* or similar in meaning like *chicken* and *rooster* give evidence of poor habits of observation or inadequate development of word recognition skills. Errors in word reading which violate the sense of the material show lack of the use of context clues. Reversals of whole words or parts of words—the reading of *saw* for *was* and *girl* for *dog*—indicate undesirable directional tendencies. Mispronunciations or failure to use the phonetic techniques the group has been taught should be noted.

Observation of a child's reading of material which has been adjusted to his ability, as in the experiment, presents a situation different from the observation of his reactions to material that is too difficult. Lack of interest or dislike for the reading may be indicative merely of his attitude toward this too difficult material rather than of his general attitude. His meager comprehension may be due to word difficulty, complexity of ideas in the material, or concepts outside his experience rather than to habitually poor comprehension. His errors in word recognition can give little indication of his use of context if the material is too difficult to permit him to form a context. Too difficult material does possess the advantage for diagnostic purposes of giving great opportunity for demonstrations of a child's habits of attack on unfamiliar words. However, these habits can be demonstrated so much more satisfactorily by use of a diagnostic test of word recognition techniques (described on pp. 67–69 of the present section) that even this reason for having any child read material that is too difficult for him is removed.

Analysis of Pupil Responses on Teaching Materials

The reading activities considered here differ from those considered above in that the pupil records his own response to a silent reading situation. Thus the teacher has records of more complete responses for more children than it would be possible for her to make through her own observation. The responses on each piece of material indicate whether the child has learned what the material was designed to teach. The points of observation noted in the above section may also be applied to pupil responses on these materials. Samples of such materials used in the experiment are here classified according to teaching aims.

Comprehension of various types of materials

1. Accuracy of reading.

    Yes-No statements based on materials previously read by the pupils and on concepts known to be familiar to all.

    > The horse likes trains.   Yes.   No.
    > The fire makes us cold.   Yes.   No.

2. Following exact directions.

    > Draw a house for a dog.
    > Put a door in the house.
    > Put two windows in the dog house.

3. Developing sentence comprehension through drawing of illustrations.

    > Peggy put the little cat on the doll's bed.

4. Developing paragraph comprehension through drawing of illustrations.

    > Sam and Blackie went out to look after the cows. They took the cows to some good green grass. The cows stopped to eat. They liked the good green grass.
    >
    > (From "Sam, the Cowboy")

5. Developing comprehension of story-size units through various types of comprehension exercises.

    Yes-No statements.

    > The horse likes trains.   Yes.   No.
    > (From "The Good Milk-man")

    Completion.

    > A boy gives Peter a red _____.
    > house   cake   box
    > (From "Peter's Birthday")

    Joining broken sentences.

    > Annie has   jumps.
    > The white dog   "See my dog jump."
    > Annie says,   a white dog.
    > (From "Annie's White Dog")

Developing word discrimination

1. Word matching with pictures.
   A picture of a tree has the word *tree* under it, followed by a group of three words among which is the word *tree* to be underlined.

   (Picture)
   t r e e

   t h r e e
   t r e e
   t r a i n

2. Same as 1, above, except that the name of the picture is not given. Word recall must be used.
3. Choice in context reading of words among those most confusable in the current vocabulary.

   house
   Peter rode on his
   horse

4. Practice in discrimination of words often mistaken for each other by means of choice words in sentences.

   on
   Baby sits   the fire.
   by

Developing the use of context clues. Many of the types of materials described above encourage the use of context in reading, especially the word selection exercises in context. The illustrations of materials are selected from those which were used in the experiment to show how teaching materials which aid in the attainment of many reading objectives may also serve as means of keeping the teacher informed of her pupils' progress.

Analysis of Pupil Responses on Diagnostic Tests

As stated previously, daily observation will supply much of the knowledge of the child's needs which the teacher must have in order to adjust his instruction. The comprehension tests which accompanied some of the supplementary reading in the experiment helped in this day-by-day adjustment. To determine levels of development, a group of tests was given after each unit of reading—usually a chapter in the textbook. The time of testing was chosen so as not to break into the continuity of instruction. These tests determined more exactly the child's development of comprehension and word recognition techniques. Illustrations of the types of tests used follow:

Vocabulary knowledge

A composite picture with names of objects above and below. Direction: "Draw a line from each word to its picture."

Sentence comprehension

Choosing the correct sentence to go with a picture.

Direction: "Draw a line under the right sentence." As the reading ability developed, Yes-No statements were used for testing sentence comprehension. These statements were based on general information related to the topics of the unit rather than on the child's memory of incidents or details in the material read.

The chickens drank the grass. Yes. No.

Direction: Draw a line under Yes or No.

Level of comprehension shown by the number of ideas in a sentence each child can read and illustrate. These sentences were given in a series beginning with the easiest. The first test given included the following illustrations to be drawn:

One idea: This is a *cat*.
Two ideas: The *house* is *brown*.
Three ideas: *Father* has a *blue book*.
Four ideas: The *dog plays* with a *red ball*.
Five ideas: *Peter gives Mother* a *red cup*.

Later tests included more ideas to a sentence.

Nine ideas: *Some boys gave* the *brown rabbit two green leaves to eat.*

Ability to discriminate between words confusable in form when clues to the word must be discovered through comprehension of the context.

been
The grass is
green

Peter sleeps in a _____.
red   did   bed

Direction: Draw a line under the right word.

APPENDIX: ADJUSTED INSTRUCTION

Word recognition techniques shown through a diagnostic test

1. Description. These tests consisted of ten or more lines of words. Each line contained five different words. The following illustration gives the first three lines of one of the tests which was used in the experiment:

horse	please	train	hen	esroh
round	drink	dnuof	found	four
her	he	me	eh	to

The child was directed to put his liner (a strip of cardboard) under the first line of words. The teacher then said, "Look all the way across and find *horse,*" or whatever word was correct for the line. Then the child drew a line under the word he had chosen. This procedure was repeated for each line.

2. Construction. To reveal the child's word recognition techniques, each line contained the correct word and four other words which were variants from the correct word according to the following classifications:

a. A reversal, as horse—esroh. (This was the only type which used any word form not in the child's reading vocabulary.)
b. A different beginning, same ending, as in horse and please.
c. A different ending, same beginning, as in horse and hen.
d. A word with the same general form as the correct word but with few or none of the same letters, as horse, train.

In the construction of the tests, the words, as they were selected, were written in column form according to these classifications. This made certain that each type of error was represented for each word:

	Error 1	Error 2	Error 3	Error 4
Correct *Word*	*Reversal*	*Wrong* *Beginning*	*Wrong* *Ending*	*Same* *Form*
horse	esroh	please	how	train
found	dnuof	round	four	drink
he	eh	me	her	to

These words were then rearranged for the final form of the test. Correct words were so distributed as to place an equal number of correct words in each of the five columns. Then type 1 words were distributed in the same way, as were types 2, 3, and 4. Care was taken that the arrangement did not affect the child's selection of the words.

After the tests were mimeographed, a key copy was made for scoring by writing on the test sheet the number classification of each error, and by underlining the correct response. For example, the three lines given above had the following classifications:

horse	please [2]	train [4]	how [3]	esroh [1]
round [2]	drink [4]	dnuof [1]	*found*	four [3]
her [3]	*he*	me [2]	eh [1]	to [4]

3. Diagnostic uses of the tests. One child's responses given below show how the classification of his errors was made, using the key above:

					Classification of errors
horse	please	train	how	esroh	1
round	drink	dnuof	*found*	four	+
her	he	me	eh	to	3

After the classification of each response, the types of errors were tabulated for each child and the individual and class summaries were made as follows:

Pupil	Total Errors	1 Reversal	2 Wrong Beginning	3 Wrong Ending	4 Same Form
1.	0	0	0	0	0
2.	4	0	3	1	0
3.	3	1	2	0	0

Each child's responses are indicative of his needs. The group summaries are diagnostic of the word recognition techniques developed by the method of teaching used.

One child marked five correct words and five incorrect ones. All the five errors were of type 3, wrong ending. They included:

soon for some
when for what
drink for draw
every for eat
or for of

Obviously this child had not developed adequate techniques of observing the final parts of words. Some children made similar errors, some made errors predominately of other types, and some made errors distributed among several types. A later section of this chapter describes the type of teaching recommended for such difficulties.

The class summaries with one group of fifteen children showed the following classification of errors on the tests for two successive chapters of the Gates-Huber Primer:

	Total Errors	1 Reversal	2 Wrong Beginning	3 Wrong Ending	4 Same Form
Chapter III	26	3	11	9	3
Chapter IV	13	8	0	5	0

The teacher made a definite effort to teach better observation of beginnings of words during the work on Chapter IV. The results of the next test—on Chapter IV—show the success of this teaching, since the number of errors classified as wrong beginnings dropped from 11 to 0. This example indicates how the class summaries on this type of test kept the teachers informed of the current needs of their pupils in habits of word recognition.

This type of test, so constructed as to show word recognition habits in relation to the child's present reading vocabulary, has been valuable as a diagnostic tool with reading defect cases outside the experiment, and with groups of children who were poor readers. Teachers seem to find it rather easy to make, and convenient to interpret.

The present section has explained how, by means of observation of pupil behavior in reading situations, and by analysis of pupil responses on teaching materials and on diagnostic tests, the teachers in the experiment kept themselves informed of their pupils' needs. The following sections will describe how these needs were met by provision of a plentiful supply of reading material and by guidance in the development of desirable reading habits. In the experiment these phases of adjustment were not separated as in the description of them. When a child's needs were discovered they were met with the necessary instruction as soon as possible. Sometimes a word or two was sufficient. Always the necessary guidance was the more effective for being given at the time it was needed. The same was true of supplementary reading. At times the basic reading material piled up difficulties more rapidly than the pupils could overcome them. On such occasions the teachers went no further with the regular reading, but gave the pupils supplementary reading experiences until they had mastered the difficulties already presented to a degree sufficient to enable them to resume the regular reading unhandicapped.

THE PROVISION OF A PLENTIFUL SUPPLY OF READING MATERIAL

It was a fundamental assumption in the experiment that the knowledges and skills which constitute reading ability are developed best by practice, in other words, by real reading. Non-reading as well as reading experiences were employed for the development of concepts and background of meaning and for guidance in the development of desirable habits or the correction of undesirable ones. However, for the development of ability to read, reliance was placed upon a plentiful amount of material which had been carefully selected or constructed according to certain standards to suit the abilities and interests of the children.

Standards of Selection and Construction of Materials

In the selection or construction of material, it was found helpful to consider four fundamental qualities of content and two qualities of presentation. The qualities of content are vocabulary, number and complexity of ideas to a sentence, the concepts involved, and the interests fostered; the qualities of presentation are mechanical arrangement and literary values.

Vocabulary. Words which the child does not know when he sees them represent for him an important factor of the difficulty of reading material. Words differ in the inherent difficulty they present to the learner. Those very similar in appearance are certain to cause difficulty if they occur in the child's reading before he has developed sufficient ability to discriminate between them. As the regular reading program controls the introduction of new words, it should take account of these factors of difficulty. Word difficulties arising from meaning are referred to in the discussion of the third fundamental quality, that of concepts. The present discussion considers the difficulties which arise when the proportion of unknown words encountered in reading becomes great in relation to the number of known words.

Unknown words are of two classes—new words and partially learned words. New words are words that have not previously occurred in the child's reading. Partially learned words are those which have occurred before in his reading but which in varying degrees fall short of becoming known words. New words in a selection under consideration may be determined readily by a comparison of the vocabulary list of the proposed material with that of the basic material. To some extent, partially learned words may be discovered in the same manner, since they are usually words most recently introduced. In any reading the child does, the presence of unknown words may be suspected from the harmful effect they have on his comprehension and fluency. Children's responses to tests and materials already described will give the teacher more precise knowledge as to what words are partially learned for each child.

New words should be introduced with care. In the main, this is the province rather of the regular than of the supplementary program, but it is the work of the latter to fill in the gaps left by the former. Any new word should be introduced in such a situation that it will make a strong impression. It should be so defined by a context of known words and, if possible, by pictures, that its right meaning is established. When new words such as "Santa Claus" and "Christmas" in the "Story of a Christmas Tree" (quoted later as an illustration of supplementary material) are used in the supplementary material the same care should be taken in presentation as with the regular material. Many such new words are of transitory need and may not be worth the many repetitions required to make them known words. In such cases, special care might be taken to depend rather on pictures and context of known words to carry the meaning of these words than on a recognition of the word form itself. There is a tendency to feel that such words do not count. Unfortunately, however, material with too great a proportion of unknown words will disorganize the reader, whether these unknown words are to become part of his sight vocabulary or are not to be used again.

Partially learned words are the special field of supplementary material. The regular reading program makes some provision for further experiences with the new words it introduces. Usually, however, these experiences are sufficient for only the most able pupils. The supplementary material provided to give these further experiences should be planned for definite partially learned words. The same procedure should be followed as with new words, placing them in a setting of known words and pictures. Comprehension exercises which accompany the reading material should be planned to show to what extent the child has become able to use these words in reading.

The objective in word learning is attained when the child has developed the ability to discriminate each new word from those words already in his reading vocabulary which resemble it most in meaning or form. With children who are learning to read, no closer discrimination than this need be expected. Adults with well-developed word recognition skills may learn a new word so thoroughly as to be able to recognize it whether it is contrasted with known words or not, but the child who has recognized "house" for some time may manifest difficulty with this known word for a time after "horse" has entered his reading vocabulary. After this discrimination has been mastered, he may have another period of difficulty with "house" after "home" has been introduced. Such confusions are not indications that the child "has a poor memory for words." They are normal signs on his part of a degree of word discrimination which was satisfactory when used with words less similar than those now confused. If handled wisely, these confusions will afford material for further development of his word recognition skills.

Supplementary material designed to meet other objectives than that of giving further experiences with partially learned words should use, in so far as possible, only familiar words. Since such material is always given for some definite purpose it should be so planned as to accomplish that purpose most effectively, unhampered by other points of difficulty. Frequently the same material may be used for different needs. However, the teacher should know for what needs she is using the given supplementary material with the individual child. In this way, while she is trying to meet the needs of each child, she will be able to keep informed of the extent to which she is meeting them.

Number and complexity of ideas to a sentence. A child may know every word in a sentence, and yet fail to understand the sentence if it contains more ideas or more complex ideas than he can grasp at once. The ability of beginners in this respect is surprisingly meager. The child may read the sentence "The black cat runs," and comprehend only what he would have comprehended from the sentence "The cat is black," or from the sentence "The cat runs." Obviously, attempts to read material that is too difficult in this respect will result in inadequate comprehension. Such reading will interfere with the development of liking for reading as well as the development of the necessary skills. The ability to grasp at one time an increasing number of ideas, and more complex ideas, develops with appropriate guidance. Samples of reading exercises which were used in the experiment to keep the teachers informed of the stage of development of their pupils in this respect were presented on page 66.

The concepts involved. These concepts are the meanings or backgrounds necessary to the reader if he is to understand the material he reads. The concepts of each individual are constantly growing with his experiences. Before he has had any experiences with cats the word "cat" means nothing to the child. Without other experience, "cat" may mean only a blob of color so named in a book at school. To a child with previous experience "cat" may mean something soft to pet, or something that makes a rumbling noise when you pet it. The concept grows as the child lives through further experiences.

Emotional qualities are added to the concept through association with a dearly loved playmate or through unhappy experiences of being scratched or frightened. As the child grows older, his concept grows still richer. The adult's concept is a vast organization of interrelated feelings and information drawn from everyday experiences, from various arts and sciences, and from other almost endless classifications of elements. It is readily apparent that the adult who is writing material for children to read must write it on the basis not of his own concepts, but of the concepts of children who are to read it if they are to understand what they read. It is possible for reading material to extend children's concepts, but this extension must grow out of the level of development which the child's concepts have already reached.

Interests fostered. Children come to school with capacities for interests rather than with fully developed interests. The interests they bring to school are a result of whatever experiences they have had before coming to school. The experiences of any one child are likely to include a relatively small number of the experiences possible to children of his age. Many of the experiences which he has not yet had might produce interests more absorbing to the child than those interests which his past experiences have developed. The school will be able to plan for the provision of such experiences.

Since there are so many possible interests, the reading program may select and foster those which are most closely related to the general aims of child development. There is no need for the choice of material whose only recommendation is that children are interested in it. Most children are interested in sensational stories of criminal adventures. They are equally interested in stories more wholesome in effect which have the same qualities of plot, suspense, and dramatic action.

Certain topics and qualities of treatment in literary materials have always interested children. The writers of enduring classics for children have, perhaps unconsciously, made their books rich in these respects. These topics and qualities have been clarified in definite statements by the studies of Dunn,[3] Gates,[4] and others.[5]

The findings of these studies have influenced the preparation of basic readers and other children's books. Certain reading materials that apparently have been constructed without regard to these findings have been planned according to a different principle of interest. They were designed to supply material from which even beginners could gather information to share in the developing of class experiences. Most basic reading materials written for use in the regular program have been planned to meet the interests of children. In varying degrees, they have succeeded.

Some groups or individual children have special interests which are not shared by others. Most of these interests, however, can be developed by other children. They are largely the result of special circumstances: the outgrowth of local industries or customs; or participation in contemporary events, seasonal activities, and holidays. Individual interests may arise from special abilities. An unusual fund of information about any topic, or skill in some activity, is usually evidence of an interest in that topic or activity which may be carried over into reading about it. A child is interested in doing what he can do well. When the reading is so adjusted to a child's ability that he enjoys a constant experience of success, this experience of success in itself fosters interest in reading.

The form of reading material has much to do with its interest. The narrative form continues to hold the interest of most children. Other forms, such as word matching, are interesting occasionally,

---

[3] F. W. Dunn, *Interest Factors in Primary Reading Material.* 1921.

[4] A. I. Gates, C. Peardon, and I. Sartorius, "Studies of Children's Interests in Reading," *Elementary School Journal,* 31:656–670, May, 1931.

[5] Forty previous studies are reviewed and original data presented in "A Survey of the Literature on the Reading Interests of Children of the Elementary Grades," *Educational Research Bulletins,* 5:2 and 3, by Sister Mary Celestine. February and March, 1930.

but prove tiresome if used constantly. Any certain form may interest some children while it seems unpleasant to others. When any child shows a dislike of certain reading material, the cause may be associated with lack of familiarity with the procedures involved, with a feeling of inferiority with relation to the performance of his classmates, or with some other factor not related to the form of the material. If the child's dislike persists after these factors have been removed, it would be wise to plan some other form of material for that child. To insure the persistence of interest, it is well to give a wide variety of forms of material, and to avoid using any one form to excess.

Mechanical arrangement. This refers to such qualities as size of type, length of line, and number and spacing of lines on a page. The supplementary material used for adjustment in the experiment followed the form used in the basic reading materials. Mimeographed materials were hand-lettered at first to conform with the style of lettering used by the teachers for blackboard and chart work. After this early period, a primer typewriter was used. The standard for mechanical arrangement by which the supplementary material was judged was the similarity of the mechanical arrangement to that of the basic material. It was assumed that any difference in arrangement would disturb some children and would introduce unnecessarily a further handicap to adjustment. The basic materials used in the experiment had been prepared in accordance with generally accepted standards of mechanical arrangement.

Some of the more important points of mechanical arrangement which were observed in the preparation of the supplementary material are:

1. The lines were not more that four inches in length.
2. Double spacing was used between lines.
3. Phrases natural in speech were kept as units on a line.
4. Thought units larger than phrases were kept on the same line so far as possible. That is, not

> Mother said, "You may go
> to the store."

but

> Mother said,
> "You may go to the store."

5. Paragraphs were indicated by indentation.
6. Paragraphs were kept as a unit, not being divided between pages.

Literary qualities. In the selection and construction of the supplementary materials used in the experiment, an attempt was made to attain the following literary qualities, in so far as they were appropriate to the purposes of the material.

1. Clarity of expression.
2. Inclusion of relevant details only.
3. Repetition, not for itself alone, but as a natural unfolding of the story.
4. Paragraphs real thought units, not merely a succession of sentences.
5. Dramatic action.
6. Suspense.
7. Climax.
8. Surprise ending.

Kinds of Supplementary Material

The three most important sources of supplementary material used in the experiment were books and other published materials, adaptations of published material, and material especially prepared for use in the experiment.

Published material. At all times during the experiment an attempt was made to keep the experimental children supplied with supplementary material which they could read with pleasure and profit. During the first months of reading, the published material which was available was too difficult to be used in this way. As each child's ability to use the available published material developed, the amount of it which he read increased. By the end of the sixth month of reading, published material was the only kind of supplementary material used for free reading. The experimental children, being potential failures, naturally progressed more slowly than average children to the point where they could read published supplementary materials. If these materials had been available in greater quantities or on levels of difficulty better suited to the abilities of these pupils, their use might have been more extensive at an earlier period. Since the completion of the experiment many such attractive and suitable easy books which would have met the standards of selection have been published. Present programs of adjustment will be aided by the use of these more recent books.

It is highly desirable to use as much published material as possible. Such materials are better than most teachers can prepare, since they are written and illustrated by experts, and have the advantage of modern methods of printing. Each year the available supply of easy material increases. Some of this material will be found to meet the standards of selection. Workbooks—both those which accompany other series of readers and those published independently—are a valuable source of supplementary material. While these workbooks cannot be used in their entirety, whole pages can be used for individual work. Further use of published materials is described later. It was considered important that all supplementary material, whether published or not, should suit the abilities and interests of the experimental group in terms of the standards of selection described previously.

Adaptation of published material. Some published material which was not suited to the abilities of the children in its published form was adapted for their use.

1. Brief books or parts of larger books which had suitable pictures but a context unsuitable for these pupils were adapted for their use by printing a suitable context on white paper and pasting it over the original context. Each page contained a large picture with a few lines of print.

2. Blank books were made from various kinds of firm paper, often brown or white wrapping paper. A series of pictures was selected and pasted on the pages, leaving room for a suitable story. This story was composed to fit the pictures and hand-lettered in India ink. Books from a five and ten cent store, particularly those containing full page photographs, were most helpful. Magazines, discarded school books and used workbooks were other sources of such pictures.

One of the stories which was written for independent reading early in the experiment is given below to illustrate this type of adaptation. The pictures were taken from a ten-cent alphabet book. They were attractive full-page photographs of children. This was one of the books that was read most at first.

Cover Page: Annie's White Dog.

Page 1. (*Picture* of a girl and a dog looking at a book)
      Context:
                    This is Annie.
                    Annie has a white dog.
                          1.

Page 2. (*Picture* of three children looking with interest at the same white dog)
Context:

> The big boy likes the dog.
> The little boy likes the dog.
> Annie likes the dog.
>
> 2.

Page 3. (*Picture* of two girls laughing and running as they hold between them a stick which the same dog is grasping in his teeth)
Context:

> The girls run.
> The dog runs.
>
> 3.

Page 4. (*Picture* of "Annie" holding something high in her hand while the white dog jumps to get it)
Context:

> The white dog jumps.
> Annie says,
> "See my dog jump."
>
> 4.

The child's ability to read this story was demonstrated by the following comprehension exercise involving the joining of broken sentences. The child was directed to draw a line from the beginning of each sentence to the part that tells the rest of the story.

Annie has	"See my dog jump."
The white dog	jumps.
Annie says,	a white dog.

3. Published pictures can be used by teachers in many ways. Large pictures increase the interest in blackboard or chart stories. Small pictures cut out and pasted on three by five inch cards make interesting reading table exercises in matching words from the reading vocabulary with appropriate pictures. Sets of pictures were made for matching with appropriate sentences, or with paragraphs such as riddles.

Sets of cards with a picture on one side and a word or sentence on the other may be used as self-teaching devices or as games to be played by small groups of children.

4. Rereading of material with a different purpose from that of the original reading is another type of adaptation which can be used with basic or supplementary material. The value of good material is not exhausted by one reading. The purposes of rereading

include, (*a*) to grasp the main points of a story or a piece of informational material for a report to the class, (*b*) to plan a dramatization, (*c*) to find out definite facts, (*d*) to settle a difference of opinion about the material, (*e*) to answer definite questions, or (*f*) to prepare to read for an audience.

Specially prepared material. As a part of the regular instruction, the teachers—as had been their custom—used chart and blackboard material for reading. Most of the specially prepared materials were mimeographed for general class use and for the reading table. Examples of various types of these materials follow.

1. Stories were written for the use of children at definite stages of development according to the vocabulary and other standards mentioned above. These stories almost always used the characters of the basic material but placed them in entirely different situations. The supplementary stories were never, either in action or in statement, repetitions of the basic material.

One such story used after the completion of the Home Unit of Chapter III in the Primer was the story of "The Fire." It is given in full below, with page divisions marked. The top half of each page was left blank for such illustrations as each child wished to draw in his own book.

The Fire.

The house is on fire!
A little girl is in bed
in the house.
Father is out.
Mother is out to get milk
for the little girl.

1

The dog is with Mother.
Peter is at school.
The house is on fire!
The little girl is in bed
in the house.

2

The little girl calls,
"Mother, it is too warm."
The little girl goes to the door
and opens it.
The fire comes in.
She runs to the bed.

3

She calls, "Mother! Mother!"
No one comes.
She calls, "Father! Father!"
No one comes.
She calls and calls.
No one comes to get her out.

4

Peter comes from school
with the boys.
Peter says,
"Our house is on fire!"
The boys run to the house.
Peter calls, "Mother,
our house is on fire!"

5

Mother comes
with milk and cakes
for the little girl.
The dog comes with Mother.
He runs to Peter.
Peter says,
"Mother, our house is on fire!"

6

Mother says,
"Baby is in the house!"
She runs to the door
and opens it.
Fire comes out.

7

A man
pulls her from the door.
She says,
"My baby is in the fire!
Please get her out."

8

Peter runs
to call the firemen.
He goes to the fire-box.
He makes the fire-box
call the firemen.

9

The firemen come.
The firemen run
to the house.

Mother calls,
"My baby is in the house!
Please get her out."
10

One fireman goes up
to the little girl's window.
He opens the window
and goes into the fire.
11

He goes to the bed.
He calls, "Baby, Baby."
The little girl comes
from under the bed.
12

The fireman puts
the little girl in a rug.
He comes out of the fire
with her.
He comes down
and gives her to Mother.
13

All the firemen
put water on the fire
and put the fire out.
14

Father comes.
He runs to Mother.
He says,
"Are all the children
out of the house?"
15

Mother says, "Yes.
All the children are here.
The good firemen
put the fire out."
Father and Mother say,
"Thank you," to the firemen.
16

This story was mimeographed on both sides of two sheets of
mimeograph paper in the following arrangement, which made it
possible to cut each sheet in half and fold the pieces to be placed

in the correct order for stapling. A blank half sheet of paper was labelled to make a cover page.

Front of Sheet 1

XXXXXXX XXXXXXX 16	XXXXXXX XXXXXXX 1 Cut
XXXXXXX XXXXXXX 14	XXXXXXX XXXXXXX 3

Back of Sheet 1

XXXXXXX XXXXXXX 2	XXXXXXX XXXXXXX 15 Cut
XXXXXXX XXXXXXX 4	XXXXXXX XXXXXXX 13

Front of Sheet 2

XXXXXXX XXXXXXX 12	XXXXXXX XXXXXXX 5 Cut
XXXXXXX XXXXXXX 10	XXXXXXX XXXXXXX 7

Back of Sheet 2

XXXXXXX XXXXXXX 6	XXXXXXX XXXXXXX 11 Cut
XXXXXXX XXXXXXX 8	XXXXXXX XXXXXXX 9

Children were encouraged to illustrate pages in this story as they desired. As a check on each child's ability to read the story with understanding, a brief set of eight true-false statements was given. The following are representative:

Mother is out to get milk.   Yes   No
The fireman puts the dog in the rug.   Yes   No

2. The form illustrated below can be made more readily by teachers, since it uses only one stencil and one side of a single sheet of

paper. This was the most popular type of material provided for the experimental groups. Of all the types used, it gave the greatest amount of reading material in proportion to the amount of time required to make it. It provides about 275 running words to a sheet of paper. When the mimeographed sheet is cut in half horizontally, the top part, folded with printing inside, makes pages 1 and 4 of a booklet. The bottom half, folded in the same way and inserted between the folded halves of the top part, forms pages 2 and 3 of the booklet. These sheets are then stapled or tied with a string, making an eight page booklet with blank pages (the backs of pages 2 and 3) opposite pages 1 and 4 for drawing pictures. The following story, "The Good Milkman," was written to be used any time after the group had read as far as page 33 of the primer. The arrangement of pages on the single sheet was as follows:

xxxxxx Fold	xxxxxx
1	4 Cut
xxxxxx	xxxxxx
2	3

The Good Milkman
A little cat and a little dog
have no breakfast.
The little cat says, "Mew-Mew.
I like milk for breakfast."
The little dog says, "Bow-wow.
I like milk for breakfast, too."
The cat and the dog
sit down and cry.
A little girl comes.
The little girl has milk
for Mother.

1

The cat says, "Mew-mew.
I like milk for breakfast."
The dog says, "Bow-wow.
I like milk for breakfast, too."
The little girl says,
"I have no milk for a cat.
I have no milk for a dog.
This milk is for Mother.
Go to the milkman, little dog.
Go to the milkman, little cat.
The milkman has milk."

The cat and the dog
go to the milkman.
The cat says to the milkman,
"Mew-mew. I like milk
for breakfast."

2

The dog says to the milkman,
"Bow-wow. I like milk
for breakfast, too."
The milkman says,
"I have milk
for boys and girls.
I have no milk
for dogs and cats."
The little cat
and the little dog
sit down and cry.

3

A train comes.
The milkman's horse runs.
He runs and runs.
He runs from the train.
The milkman runs
after the horse.
The milkman calls, "Here! Here!"
He says,
"Please get the horse, little dog.
Please get the horse."
The little dog
runs after the horse.
He says, "Bow-wow! Bow-wow!"
The little cat runs, too.
The horse comes
to the milkman.

> The milkman says,
> "I have milk for a good little dog.
> I have milk for a good little cat.
> Here is milk for breakfast."
>
> 4

Ability to read the story with understanding was demonstrated by responses to six true-false statements based on the story. Two examples are given:

> The dog says, "I like trains for breakfast." Yes No
> The milkman has milk. Yes No

Only very easy questions were used. When this type of story was used in the very early part of the work, it seemed best to have only a few lines on a page.

3. Stories for special occasions were written to meet the interests of those occasions. These stories were expected to follow as closely as any other supplementary material the standards of construction of reading materials described above. The story illustrated here included three words which were not in the pupils' vocabulary. A picture of a Christmas tree on the front cover page with the title of the story identified the words Christmas Tree. A picture of Santa Claus on the back cover page holding a card on which was printed,

> Santa Claus says,
> "This book is for
> _____ "

identified the term Santa Claus. The third word, "Purr," was used in a suggestive context. At the time this story was read the pupils had completed the reading of the first 26 pages of the Primer. The total vocabulary of their school reading material was 78 words. The ease with which the pupils read this story may account for the keen interest which the teachers reported.

The "Story of a Christmas Tree" was, like "The Good Milkman," put on a single stencil. It made a booklet with eight pages of printed material. The backs of the printed pages formed four blank pages for drawing pictures. This booklet was in a popular size which fitted the pockets of first grade children. After reading his book, each child wrote his name on the line on the back cover and was given the booklet for his own library.

The story is given on the following page in the form in which it was prepared:

	Fold	

(Picture of Santa Claus holding the card which h a s   t h e words:)
 	
    Santa Claus, says,
    "This book is for
    _____."
		The Story of a
		Christmas Tree
		
		(Picture of
		a
		Christmas Tree)

Cut

Peggy says,
"The little bed is my bed.
What is on my bed?"

    The little cat says,
"Purr, purr."

6

I am a Christmas Tree.
I am in Peter's house.
I am green.
I have little blue balls.
I have little red balls.
I am on a big red rug.
This is my story.

I

Cut

It is morning.
The children come
to the Christmas Tree.

Peter says,
"This is my train."

5

Night comes.
The children go to bed.

2

Cut

The Mother cat comes.
She has a baby cat.
She puts the baby cat
on the little bed.

4

Fold

Santa Claus comes.
Santa Claus puts a train
under the Christmas Tree.
The train is for Peter.

3

4. Other stories similar to those above were written, each page containing a brief paragraph illustrated by a picture to be colored.

5. Some stories were written in the form of comic strips. The single sheet was mimeographed lengthwise, and was divided into six sections—three at the top and three at the bottom. In each of the six sections a large space was left for a drawing to illustrate the reading material printed at the bottom. In the space for the picture in some of these cartoons, balloons were mimeographed containing

the conversation of the characters. The children were to draw a line from the mouth of the character to the appropriate balloon. The example below had balloons in three of the sections.

XXXXXXX 1	XXXXXXX 2	XXXXXXX 3
XXXXXXX 4	XXXXXXX 5	XXXXXXX 6

The story follows:

A big boy gives a box
to the big brown dog.
The big boy says,
"The box is for the children."

1

The big brown dog
comes to the door with the box.
The dog says, "Bow-wow."

2

The door opens.
The big brown dog
comes in with the box.

3

The big brown dog
gives the box to the children.
Here is the box.
Here are the children.

4

The girl opens the box.
A little cat is in the box.
The little cat says, "Mew-mew."

5

The little cat runs.
The big brown dog
runs after the little cat.

6

6. A type of material which is more economical of stencils, though not of children's reading time, fills each stencil with reading material which is to be cut apart and pasted into booklets made of unlined first grade paper. One sheet of paper folded once crosswise makes a four page booklet. The children paste on each page the appropriately numbered reading material. Then they draw illustrations for the story. This type requires more guidance at first than do the types described previously. The experimental children worked with it successfully from the beginning of book reading. The illustration given was used during the reading of Chapter IV of the Primer.

Make a book of this story.

The farmer milked the cow.

I

The brown chicken drank the milk.

2

The black dog
ran after the brown chicken.

3

The farmer took the milk
to the house.

4

7. Stories with an obvious sequence were mimeographed without page numbers. Consequently it was necessary for the children to read to determine the order of the paragraphs before pasting them on the pages of their booklets.

8. Exact directions for drawing pictures were used occasionally. These directions were simple at first, and grew more complicated as the children's ability developed.

Draw a white house.
Put two windows in the house.
Make the windows yellow.
Draw one door in the house.
Make the door blue and yellow.

9. Type 8 was varied to give practice in exact discrimination of confusable words.

> Draw a house and a horse.
> Put an X on the house.

10. Confusable words were presented as choice words in sentences.

> The cat _____ "Mew-mew."
>   sits
>   says

11. Confusable words were presented with a picture. The child drew a line under the right word from a list of two or three such words. Care was taken to vary the type of confusable words used together. Usually the list contained the right word and two other words from the child's reading vocabulary—one with a different beginning and one with a different ending.

> (Picture of Mother)
> Morning
> Father
> Mother

12. Miniature charts for the reading table were constructed in a form similar to the wall charts that are sometimes used for displaying word and sentence cards for group reading. A piece of typewriter paper was folded so as to form about seven pleats one inch apart and one-fourth inch deep. A piece of tag board nine by twelve inches was used as a backing sheet. The edges of the tag board were folded forward and stapled to hold the typewriter sheet in place. A wide space was left above the top pleat for the insertion of pictures or other material. The material for each exercise was placed in an envelope. In each case, the envelope contained pictures, words, phrases, or sentences on two or three rectangles of paper about three inches high to be placed in the top pleat of the chart. Slips one inch high containing words, phrases, or sentences were supplied to be placed in the lower pleats matching the appropriate headings.

One such exercise for early reading provided a picture of the cat the children were reading about in the story in the basic reader with the name "Twinkle" underneath, and a picture of Peter's dog with the name "Tags" underneath. This large piece of paper was inserted in the top fold. There were ten to fourteen of the one-inch slips containing sentences about the dog and sentences about the cat. These sentences were not like the sentences in the Primer though they were necessarily restricted to the vocabulary of the Primer. The direction on the envelope was,

> Make a story about Tags.
> Make a story about Twinkle.

The sentences to be arranged under the picture were on separate slips of paper. They included such statements as

> I have milk in a blue cup.
> I am a big dog.
> I am white.

and others. After having selected the sentences to go under each heading, the child rearranged them to make the stories sound more interesting.

The chart has several advantages over material to be laid on the desk. It holds the material in a good position for reading and re-reading. It can be saved for checking at the teacher's convenience. It can be used to meet individual needs and interests. With the experimental groups, the names of all the children who seemed to need any particular exercise were written on the envelope which contained the materials for that exercise, and checked off as these children completed it. The other children used the materials as they wished. By use of envelopes containing exercises as described above, many types of reading can be provided in addition to those used in the experiment, which included (a) colors matched with colors, (b) words matched with colors, (c) words matched with pictures, (d) phrases matched with pictures, (e) sentences matched with pictures, and (f) sentences grouped under pictures.

13. A series of hand-lettered and illustrated booklets was supplied for the reading table during the earliest period of book reading. One of these booklets was "The Ball Book." This booklet was made of one sheet of colored construction paper and three sheets of unlined first grade paper. These sheets were folded and tied or stapled. On the cover was pasted a circular piece of colored construction paper and the title, "The Ball Book." The first page contained a picture of a red ball and the sentence, "This is a red ball." On the succeeding pages were pictures of balls of blue, white, yellow, brown, and black, with a sentence for each, "This is a blue ball," "This is a white ball," etc. Similar booklets were made with the titles, "The Boy Book," "The Girl Book," "The Dog Book," and "The Cat Book." Each booklet was accompanied by a simple exercise in

which the child read a sentence quoted from the booklet and colored appropriately an outline drawing. These booklets are useful only in the beginning stages of reading, when children are learning what it means to read. They were so greatly enjoyed by the experimental children that the sets supplied each group were completely worn out.

Mimeographed materials were used extensively to supplement the basic material in the experiment for the following reasons: (a) Since of all the types that were constructed, mimeographed materials were most similar to book reading, they required less adjustment on the part of the children and presumably facilitated their learning; (b) individual differentiation of instruction could be made more easily when each child had a copy of the material; (c) several teachers were being supplied with the same materials; (d) children had booklets for their own personal "libraries"; (e) children could take home to read to parents materials which they could read successfully; and (f) it was possible to keep files of children's work to watch their progress.

When facilities for mimeographing are limited or not available, some of the advantages of mimeographed materials can be provided by blackboard and chart materials. For example, the longer stories may be hand-lettered or lettered with a rubber stamp printing set on tag board and hung in a series along the wall of the classroom for group reading. These same large sheets of tag board might be made into a "big book." Such exercises as the choice words in sentences and directions to draw may be placed on the blackboard. Children can illustrate the cartoon or comic strip type of story by folding their papers into six parts, numbering the parts, and drawing the appropriate pictures according to the story on the blackboard. The group rereading of the story might result in selection of the best pictures to paste on a "comic strip" for the reading table. This "comic strip" might be prepared in advance with the story printed by the teacher, spaces having been left for the children's drawings.

Uses of Supplementary Material

A consideration of the contribution which reading materials can make to the general development of children should guide the choice of content of these materials. The uses of these materials in providing social experiences among members of the group should be guided by the teacher's knowledge of the principles of social development in children. Each child's experiences in relation to the reading material will, to a great extent, determine his attitudes toward reading. His relation to his teacher in reading situations is equally influential. Obviously, the program of adjustment shares these responsibilities with the regular program.

The supplementary materials used in the experiment were relatively small in quantity, probably less than the "seat work" materials made by many teachers. For the most part, each piece of material was capable of affording practice in more than one skill. Guidance by the teacher, it was planned, would so emphasize the type of practice needed in each case that this material would have the effectiveness of a greater amount of material not so guided. It was believed that when the child was conscious of the aim of his reading activity, he would be able to accomplish this aim by reading a smaller amount of material than he would need if he read without being conscious of the aim. The results of the experiment seem to show that according to these assumptions supplementary material may be used with success. This guided use of materials has the practical advantage of providing an adequate amount of practice without requiring a prohibitive amount of material.

The uses of supplementary material in the experiment were of two kinds, reading to meet a specific need, and reading for general development and enjoyment. The former will be referred to as directed reading, the latter as free reading.

Directed reading. The uses of materials for directed reading are listed below according to the reading abilities which they aim to develop. The fostering of interests and the maintenance of desirable attitudes are general aims which should be present in all reading.

1. Comprehension of story-length units. Reading activities used to develop this ability include:

(*a*) Rereading with a new purpose (pages 78–79).

(*b*) Group discussion of stories, which often results from or motivates such rereading.

(*c*) Answering comprehension questions which require a general knowledge of the story.

(*d*) Drawing illustrations for large units of a story.

2. Comprehension of paragraph units:

(*a*) Matching pictures with riddles.

(*b*) Illustrating riddles.

(*c*) Illustrating one page paragraphs of mimeographed stories (pages 85–86).

(*d*) Illustrating the "comic strip" type of story (pages 86–87).

(*e*) Following exact directions for drawing pictures (pages 88–89).

(*f*) Arranging cut-out sentences in paragraphs according to sequence.

3. Comprehension of sentence units:

(*a*) Following sentence directions.

(*b*) Illustrating sentences.

(*c*) Answering Yes-No exercises.

(*d*) Joining broken sentences to show comprehension of material read (page 64).

(*e*) Completing a sentence by underlining the correct one of two or three choice words (page 64).

(*f*) Playing reading table games with sentence cards (page 78).

(*g*) Arranging cut out sentences in paragraphs according to sequence.

4. Increasing the level of comprehension in terms of the number and complexity of ideas per sentence. Many of the types of materials suggested under "Comprehension of sentence units" were used to develop this ability. Probably the best means of increasing the level of comprehension is to select material within the child's ability, and to raise the level gradually as his ability improves. Obviously, it is necessary to keep constantly informed as to his present ability.

5. Reading for exact details. This type of comprehension can be developed by means of those materials listed under paragraph and sentence comprehension which require knowledge of exact details rather than a general impression. This includes:

(*a*) Illustrating the "comic strip" type of story.

(*b*) Following exact directions for drawing pictures.

(*c*) Illustrating sentences.

(*d*) Answering Yes-No exercises.

(*e*) Completing sentences by underlining the correct one of two or three choice words.

(*f*) Rereading by each child to check the accuracy of his response to such reading.

6. Increasing the vocabulary of sight words:

(*a*) Reading material in which the word to be learned appears in a context of familiar words.

(*b*) Reading the partially learned vocabulary in work-type and story material.

(*c*) Reading table materials for matching words with pictures and sentences with pictures.

(*d*) Developing better word perception habits.

(*e*) During the experiment, teachers were advised to use the reading of the vocabulary in meaningful context rather than isolated word drills as a means to vocabulary teaching.

7. Use of the context to aid in the recognition of unfamiliar words:

(*a*) When the teacher has guided the child to an awareness of the value of this skill, almost all reading material of sentences or larger units will give practice in it.

(*b*) Completing sentences in which the cue to the right word is in the meaning of the sentence.

(*c*) Any means which improves comprehension increases the amount of context the child may use as clues to an unfamiliar word.

8. Improvement in discrimination of word forms. Training in this ability should rarely if ever be given during shared reading experiences; it belongs rather in the individual study-reading. Guidance can be very effective in the development of this ability. In the experiment, it was believed that the materials to develop discrimination of word forms were most effective when they afforded practice after guidance had been given according to individual and group needs. The types of materials used include:

(*a*) Following exact directions for drawing pictures when the name of the objects to be drawn were confusable words (page 89).

(*b*) Completing sentences when the choice words were confusable in form (page 89).

(*c*) Choosing from among two or three words similar in form, the right word to go with a picture (page 89).

Further means of developing word discrimination were so much more a matter of guidance than of materials that they will be discussed in the next section.

Free reading. Enjoyment of independent reading is the most certain indication of good comprehension. Providing the reader with many types of material at a level of difficulty which permits enjoyment is one of the means of insuring good comprehension. Samples of such materials used in the experiment are given on pages 79–86. These stories were written for the period before the pupils could read any of the available published material or supplementary books. The instructions sent to the teachers with the first group of these stories is quoted in part:

"The aim is to read for the pleasure of reading, without any study aim; to develop independence by unaided reading of material without vocabulary difficulties; to develop the desire to read for its own sake, not as a preparation for oral reading. To attain these aims, it will be necessary to have stories with little or no vocabulary difficulty. Any anticipated vocabulary difficulties will be taken care of outside this free reading period. If many are anticipated, then the material is so difficult as to defeat the purpose of the reading. The reading will at all times be done silently first, in sections long enough to satisfy the reader's interest in the incidents of the story. Each child will read at his own rate, never waiting for the slower readers, and having a new book as soon as he has satisfied his interest in the old one and given some evidence that he has read the book competently. No introductory remarks which give away the point of the story should be made. After the silent reading, children who complete the reading of a book at about the same time will enjoy getting together in groups of three or more and reading it orally together. When each child decides he is ready for group reading, he can best show his competence by answering the comprehension questions prepared for that story."

At this early period, each child was given a comprehension exercise after each book he read. The purpose of this exercise was to give both to his teacher and to him evidence that he had read the book competently. It seemed wise, too, to give the child this help in developing reading habits. After children become competent readers, such an exercise at the end of each piece of material read might discourage the wide reading which is desirable.

One means which was used to encourage independent reading in this early period was a rectangle drawn in the form of a book to be folded to look like a book. This rectangle was cut out by the child, colored, and pasted after his name in a square on a wall chart as soon as he had completed the exercise satisfactorily. This device proved valuable during the early reading.

As soon as each child was able to read the available published material with pleasure and profit, he was encouraged to do so. By the time the children had acquired this ability they no longer needed the guidance of comprehension exercises following each piece of material. They talked informally with their teachers about the books they were reading. It was believed that at this time the developing interest in reading and progress in reading ability could be fostered best by giving the children opportunities for wide reading of books of their own selection. The success of such reading is dependent to a great degree upon the provision of a number and variety of suitable books readily accessible for individual reading. In addition to the regular free reading period, when all the children enjoyed the activities of the reading table, the pupils were encouraged to read independently whenever they did not need the instruction being given their group.

Amount of Supplementary Material Needed

The amount of supplementary material needed in the adjustment of any reading program to the abilities of the children will vary with the effectiveness of the basic program, with the skill of the teacher, and with the reading abilities of the children. In planning the amount and kind of supplementary material needed, previous experience with the basic material is very helpful. The following suggestions are based on the experience of carrying out the experimental program.

The workbook of the basic materials was used. Had it not been used, a great deal more of the specially constructed supplementary material would have been necessary.

The amount of additional supplementary material needed at each point seemed to be proportionate to the amount of preparatory material provided by the workbook at that point.

The greatest amount of supplementary material was needed with the first unit of the basal material. The amount necessary decreased gradually until very little was needed with Chapter V of the Primer.

Supplementary material was needed by these slow groups at the introduction of each new technique and type of material.

Supplementary material was necessary whenever many new words were introduced close together in the basic reader.

It was found desirable to prepare, for each unit in the Primer, at least one supplementary story written with the new words of the unit in a context of well-known words from previous units. This story could be used for directed reading as needed. If not needed for directed reading, it was available for free reading.

It was found advisable to prepare most of the material a unit ahead, noting for future consideration materials that seemed appropriate for later levels of development.

Any part of the program of adjustment could be used independ-

ently of any other part. For example, faulty habits of word recognition might be discovered through use of the diagnostic test described on pages 67–69, and the necessary guidance and practice given, whether or not the rest of the program was being used.

Responsibility for Provision of Supplementary Material

In the experiment, the supplementary material was provided by the experimenter. In practice, it is neither necessary nor desirable for any teacher, through her own efforts alone, to supply all of the supplementary material needed by her pupils. Much of the material after the early reading—perhaps the middle of the Primer—can be found in published materials which might be supplied by the school. Cooperation among the teachers in a free exchange of materials would lighten the amount of work necessary for each teacher. The administration of the school could greatly facilitate such an exchange at a saving of expense. In any case, these supplementary materials should, for each class, meet the standards of selection and construction described previously in this section. Diagnostic tests should probably be constructed by each teacher for her own group, or for each basic vocabulary.

Even in a one-teacher rural school, the teacher can arrange with teachers of other schools to divide the work and to share knowledge and materials. If the teacher feels that she must provide all the supplementary material herself, perhaps it would be best for her to try to supply only a part of it each year, in such form that she can accumulate these materials for future use.

GUIDANCE

Guidance, as understood in the experiment, means the directing of the learner's attack on reading material in such a way as to promote the development of desirable attitudes and skills. This implies that the teacher has means of keeping informed as to the pupils' level of development and as to the techniques they are using. It implies that she has materials or other means of instruction available to develop those skills which need more practice than the regular program provides. These means and materials have been discussed fully in the two preceding sections. The present section will be devoted to the direct instruction which precedes or accompanies the use of such materials. This guidance may take two forms, initiatory and corrective.

Initiatory Guidance

Initiatory guidance consists of direct instruction which is given to the group as a whole at the introduction of any new material or technique in which many of the pupils are certain to need help. It may consist of explanations or demonstrations by the teacher and some supervised practice. The purpose of this type of guidance is to make reasonably certain that good techniques are practiced from the beginning.

This type of guidance belongs rather to the basic reading program than to the program of adjustment. However, when the basic program has neglected to provide such guidance, the adjusted program must supply it.

Unless the teacher keeps closely informed of her pupils' needs, there is some danger that this type of guidance will waste the time of some of the pupils who do not need the explanations. There is an even greater danger that this guidance will not be adequate for the needs of the slower-learning pupils.

Corrective Guidance

Corrective guidance consists of direct instruction given after needs have been discovered through the use of such means as those described previously. Such guidance is given in small groups or individually to those children who have shown a need for it. It differs from initiatory guidance in that the child who needs help is conscious of the exact nature of his need and what he must do to meet it.

Some of the attitudes and skills whose desirable development can be furthered by guidance are considered below. Since some of these have been described in previous sections of this Appendix, the present consideration will be brief and confined in so far as possible to points not considered elsewhere.

Interests and attitudes. Interests and desirable attitudes should be furthered by every reading experience. The teacher can exercise guidance in these respects by being sensitive to the attitudes of her pupils, by being enthusiastic in her praise of good work and unobtrusive in her corrective guidance, and by enjoying with the children what they read.

Comprehension. Comprehension of various types has been discussed in detail elsewhere. Often pupils need guidance in developing certain types of comprehension though they may be quite competent in others. The greatest contribution which a teacher can make to comprehension is the development in her pupils of an ideal of accuracy. She will give them opportunities to practice this accuracy in different types of comprehension and opportunities to know to what extent they have succeeded.

Reading vocabulary. The emphasis in the experiment was on the acquisition of desirable skills for attack on new words and for recognition of old ones. The number of words in a child's sight vocabulary was considered to be a natural consequence of the development of these skills rather than an aim in itself. Accordingly, guidance usually took the forms described below for the development of word recognition skills. Isolated word drills were not used.

Use of context to aid in word recognition. Opportunity for the use of context is present from the beginning of a child's reading. It is the place of guidance to see that this use is developed into an effective skill. Use of context is one type of comprehension. Therefore means that develop comprehension can also be employed to improve the use of context. In the following example of informal means to develop skill in the use of context, the similarity to the completion type of comprehension exercise will be noted. The teacher presents a sentence of known words with one word covered. The child reads the rest of the sentence and guesses the covered word. Then he reads the complete sentence to check his guess. In early uses of this teaching technique, especially, the sentence should make the missing word obvious to insure development of the skill and to avoid possible confusions.

Directional skills. From the very beginning good reading is characterized by a left-to-right observation of reading materials. The need for this directional skill in sentence material is so obvious that teachers usually provide for it.

The need for the left-to-right attack on single words is as great, although it is more commonly neglected by the basic reading instruction. Use of the diagnostic test described on pages 67–69 readily indicates directional habits that have resulted in errors of word recognition. Incorrect directional attack has been found to yield with surprising ease in many cases to simple explanation and demonstration such as, "We always look across a word like this," drawing the finger under the word from left to right, and pronouncing it, removing the finger and again drawing it under the word from left to right, and pronouncing it. This demonstration is accompanied by the explanation that when we have to look at a word more than once, we look at it that way every time.

Developing word-form discrimination. In the experiment, major emphasis was placed on the use of context clues for word recognition. It was believed that exclusive emphasis on word form clues tends to develop slow word-by-word reading. The technique most generally used in the experiment to encourage word-form discrimination was as follows: The confused words were placed one over the other; the pupil pronounced both and described in what way they were different; then he pronounced both again, emphasizing the difference in sound. If he continued to confuse the words, he was given supplementary material in the form of sentences, the completion of which depended upon a choice between the two words. For example,

Peggy goes to school with the   chicken.
                                          children.

The pupil underlined the correct word. Sometimes he was aided in his discrimination between the words by pictures illustrating the two difficult words—in the example given, a picture of some children with the word children under it and a picture of a chicken with the word chicken under it. It was believed that conscious observation of the differences and similarities between words rather than repetition was the mode of learning.

Guidance in Writing, Spelling, and Phonics

The word-study habits developed in writing and spelling work greatly affect the word-study habits pupils will use in reading. Many programs for the teaching of spelling and writing completely disregard this effect. It is desirable that the program of adjusted instruction in reading inquire into the effects of the writing and spelling programs, and modify so far as possible features harmful to progress in reading. In the experiment, the spelling and writing programs were modified according to the plan described below.

Method of teaching writing and spelling. The following bulletin given to the teachers of this experiment describes a method of teaching writing and spelling planned to aid rather than to interfere in the development of habits of word study desirable for reading.

There are at least three memories which a learner can use to help him spell a word.

1: The memory of the letter names in the right order for that word.

2: The memory of the appearance of the word, either as a whole or part by part.

3: The memory of the sounds of the word translated into letters.

The teacher, by the tasks she gives the learner to do to insure his learning, sets to a great degree which of these three memories he will use in his learning. Oral spelling almost certainly guarantees the use of the first without the second or third. In written spelling it is possible for a learner to use any one of the three without the other two. If he says the letters of the word orally before he writes, he has already guided his learning toward the first type of memory, but will often, though not always, derive some help from the second type of memory.

Let us consider these three types of memory for words in their relation to the other word-study activities required of school children.

In reading, we want children for the most part to use the memory for the appearance of the word. The rapid recognition of words from their appearance is the only means by which a child can become a fluent reader. If he can use the sounds of the letters, putting them together to make a word when he does not recognize it instantly "at sight" or from its appearance, we approve. But if he must stop to sound many words in reading the material of his grade, we do not consider his reading habits good. Nor can a child acquire an adequate knowledge of phonics to enable him to read by this method alone. If he names the letters of words to read them, we consider his habits of word recognition very bad. To summarize the generally accepted beliefs concerning desirable types of memory for learning words to read them, Type 2 is the most desirable. Type 3 has some helps for reading, but Type 1 is definitely undesirable.

Since the difference between good writing and poor writing is a difference of letter and word form, the concentration on form of letters and words would seem to induce better writing than concentration upon letter names. The testimony of many teachers is that it does. Type 2, then, which is the memory for the form of the word, gives the greatest help to writing. Type 1 makes the procedure more complex by keeping the attention of the writer centered, not upon the form of the letters or words, but upon their names. Type 3 seems to have little to offer.

There is a second advantage to the learner's concentration on the form of the word as he writes it. His mental picture can be compared with what he has written and, in this way, he can make that quick check upon the accuracy of his written word form which we know is characteristic of good spellers. As the writing process becomes more complex and the child goes beyond the stage of writing dictated sentences, he must spend an increasingly greater proportion of his effort upon the meaning of what he is writing and less and less upon the writing itself. It is a common experience that children who are good writers in second grade become poorer writers in fourth, when the content requirement of their writing receives their greatest attention. That is the time when the child particularly needs this ability to think of the word form as he writes it. If, from the beginning, he has thought of the word form as he wrote, the danger of his writing habits breaking down under this change of emphasis will be lessened.

In order to develop the "spelling sense" which enables a person to be a good speller, one of the greatest needs is the ability to translate word sounds into letters. The way the spelling words are taught either ignores or aids the development of this ability. It is the ability which enables the learner to use the memory for a word mentioned in Type 3. It is interesting to note that children learning to write Italian, which is a purely phonetic language, do not study spelling. They do not need it. It is desirable, then, that our method of teaching spelling develop the child's ability to translate word sounds into letters. From it, he derives help for both reading and spelling. Which lends itself better to this development, naming the letters as he writes, or saying the word sounds and thinking of the word form as he writes the letters? It seems justifiable to believe that if the child says the word sounds as he writes the letters, he *is* translating word sounds into letters, and by such constant practice, develops desirable phonetic abilities for both reading and spelling.

Phonics as a method of word study for reading can obviously be helped by the kind of memory for spelling described in Type 3. Indeed, every word written is a lesson in associating letters with letter sounds, when the writer pronounces the word part by part as he writes it. Difficulties in blending known sounds are encountered often in reading. The word *string*, for example, may cause difficulty even when the sounds of the word parts *s, t, r,* and *ing* are known. By practicing the prolonged sounding of word parts as he writes them, the child is giving a slow blending of those sounds such as we want for his attack upon unrecognized words in reading.

There is undoubtedly a close relation between accuracy of pronunciation and accuracy of spelling. The memory for the sounds of a word mentioned in Type 3 emphasizes, or even compels, accuracy of pronunciation. This memory for sounds combined with Type 2, the memory of the word form, clears up such spelling and pronunciation difficulties as are encountered in the words *pitcher* and *picture*.

There are, then, at least five purposes of word study for school children: for spelling; for the rapid recognition of words in reading; for phonics, a secondary purpose—to aid in the working out of words in reading when the rapid recognition fails or the word is new; for writing; and for speaking. The types of memory for spelling have been considered in relation to each of these. It appears that Type 1 is of service for spelling alone, and that, even there, it is not the type of memory best suited to spelling as it will be used in the writing of original sentences. It is a definite handicap if used in reading. It has little effect upon the other three purposes. Type 2, the memory of the appearance of the word, is of help for all five. Type 3, the memory of the word sounds translated into letters, is of service in spelling whenever any part of a word is spelled phonetically, and it helps in phonics and in pronunciation. Our aim in the teaching of spelling, if it is to be most effective, will consider the interrelationships of the habits the children establish in all their word-study activities, and will set the spelling tasks of the learners to result in the memories of Type 2 and Type 3 rather than of Type 1.

A word should never be taught as a spelling word without first giving it a meaningful setting. The belief that a word is best learned for spelling and reading by a recall of the visible word form is not new in educational literature. It is the basis of many of the activities of the workbooks to be used with the reading books. Three of the most capable students of reading defects—Gates, Gray and Monroe, use the comparison of word forms as a regular procedure to bring about a more accurate observation and recall.

GENERAL PLAN FOR TEACHING SPELLING TO ENCOURAGE THE MEMORY OF THE WORD FORM AND THE USE OF LETTER SOUNDS

Practice writing all the letters to be used in the new words and any letters that have seemed difficult in the old words.

Tell the children the word to be spelled and give them a sentence as a sample which is as suggestive as possible of its meaning.

Put the word on the board as you want the children to write it, saying the word parts as you write them. (Not the letter names, but sounds.) It is very important that you say the sound *as* you write it. For example, in writing the word *so,* you would write s as you say the sound of s and write o as you say the sound of o. In no other way can the phonics and the spelling help each other.

Ask the children to use the word in sentences. They will not all listen to a great many sentences. Four or five seem to be the limit.

A. (Study) Ask the children to say the word slowly with you as you draw your hand under the word from left to right, pausing slightly under each letter as you say its sound. (This is for beginners with two or three letter words. With the older children the unit will be syllables or word parts like *ing.*)

Say it together again, asking them this time to look at the word carefully so that they can remember how it looks.

Tell them, "Now we are going to write it. Take another good look at it so that you will be sure to write it correctly."

B. (Write without looking at a copy.) Have the papers prepared in advance, so that each child has a paper appropriate for his class and age for the writing and a smaller paper to cover the written words. His pencil should be of such a size that he can write comfortably. If it is too short to rest against the flesh between the joints of his thumb and forefinger it will cause a cramped writing and too much concentration on the writing process to allow sufficient thought for the word form.

After the children are in writing position, have them again look at the word to remember how it looks as you draw your hand under it and say it slowly together.

Say to them, "Write the word, _____. Let me hear you say it as you write it." Say the word slowly with them. Each child should be saying aloud the word part he is writing. (Not letter names.)

C. (Check it and mark it right or wrong.) When all have finished writing, have them check the word by comparison with the one on the board. Have them notice particularly in your accurate copy on the board any part of the word which was difficult for them.

Go through steps A, B, and C three times. Children who have made errors should write until they have three correct words. Errors are not common with this method.

If you are to follow step B as planned (write without looking at a copy), it will be necessary for the child at each writing of the word to cover any previous copies he has written. Otherwise he can merely copy the word, not depending on his memory at all. For this purpose a second piece of paper about three inches by five inches can be used. Have him cover the previous copy as soon as he has checked it, so that the second study and writing of the word will not be interrupted.

If the several copies of the word are written in column form, the child's comparison for checking will be facilitated as will his comparison for improved quality of writing.

Have the children close their eyes and try to "see" the word, or try to remember how it looks. As they try to visualize the word, have them say it softly together to help their recall.

It may help in the learning of the letters to have them read the letters of the words they have written, either for each checking or after the word has been written three times.

Words should be reviewed often. If your spelling lesson has been two words, the first should be written again after the second and before the final checking of the day's learning.

Include in your testing of the day's work the writing of some of the letters. This can be dropped as soon as children write all the letters without hesitation. It should be continued at intervals.

As soon as the spelling vocabulary will allow it, some sentences should be written without a copy, but only very short ones using only the words best known. It is far more difficult for a child to write a word in a sentence than in a list. You do not want any practicing of errors.

The spelling program described above would not necessarily interfere in any way with the spontaneous writing of material while carrying out other activities, since, in those activities, first grade children are not expected to be able to write the words from memory. It should, however, give them a better method of attack on words for this purpose than the copying of single letters, one after another, which many first grade children do in writing words.

Method of teaching phonics. It was not considered advisable to teach much phonics to first grade children, especially such slow learners as those who participated in the experiment. To facilitate the use of letter sounds for spelling, the words taught together often contained similar sounds. The teachers were asked to direct the children's attention to these similarities of sound and form in the words.

SUMMARY

1. In this Appendix materials have been presented and techniques described by which instruction was successfully adjusted to a group

of children who, at the beginning of first grade, were potential failures.

2. Adjusted instruction was, for the purposes of this experiment, defined as that part of a complete reading program which so supplements any basic program as to meet continuously the needs of each individual while it conserves the social and practical values of group teaching. The aim of the program of adjustment is to make it possible for each child to participate successfully in the complete reading program. It does not seek to take the place either of the basic program or of the program of wide and varied reading.

3. The teacher who wishes to employ adjusted instruction needs to have definitely in mind the objectives of her regular program. She needs practical means of keeping continuously informed concerning the degree to which each child is attaining these objectives. She needs to have ready for use a plentiful supply of reading materials to meet the needs of her pupils as she discovers them. She needs to have available techniques of guidance in the development of desirable skills for reading.

BIBLIOGRAPHY

ALABAMA DEPARTMENT OF EDUCATION. Research and Survey Series, Number 44, *Survey of Conecuh County Schools.* 1932.

BENNETT, A. "Launching a Reading Project," Part I. *Journal of Exceptional Children,* 5:82–86, 93, January, 1939.

BETTS, E. A. *The Prevention and Correction of Reading Difficulty.* Row, Peterson, and Company, Evanston, Ill., 1936.

BLANCHARD, PHYLLIS. "Reading Disabilities in Relation to Maladjustment." *Mental Hygiene.* 12:772–788, October, 1928.

BOND, EVA. *Reading and Ninth Grade Achievement.* Contributions to Education, No. 756. Bureau of Publications, Teachers College, Columbia University, New York, 1938.

BOND, G. L. *The Auditory and Speech Characteristics of Poor Readers.* Contributions to Education, No. 657, Bureau of Publications, Teachers College, Columbia University, New York, 1935.

BUHLER, C. "The Social Behavior of the Child." *Handbook of Child Psychology* (C. Murchison, ed.). Clark University Press, Worcester, Mass., 1931.

CELESTINE, Sister MARY. "A Survey of the Literature on the Reading Interests of Children of the Elementary Grades." *Educational Research Bulletins,* 5:2 and 3. The Catholic Education Press, Catholic University of America, Washington, D. C., 114p. February and March, 1930.

COOPER, I. M. "Comparative Study of the Organization for the Teaching of Ten Beginning Reading Systems." *Journal of Educational Research,* 28:347–357, January, 1935.

DE LONG, V. R. "Primary Promotion by Reading Levels." *Elementary School Journal,* 38:663–671, May, 1938.

DEPUTY, E. C. *Predicting First Grade Reading Achievement.* Contributions to Education, No. 426. Bureau of Publications, Teachers College, Columbia University, New York, 1930.

DOLCH, EDWARD W. "The Efficiency of Primers in Teaching Word Recognition." *Journal of Educational Research,* 28:271–275, December, 1934.

DOLCH, E. W. AND BLOOMSTER, M. "Phonic Readiness." *Elementary School Journal,* 38:201–205, November, 1937.

DUNKLIN, H. "How a Group of Reading Failures Was Taught to Read." Unpublished Manuscript. 1934.

DUNKLIN, L. *Summary of the Report on Remedial Reading for the Year 1934–35.* Board of Education, Buffalo, N. Y.

DUNKLIN, L. *Special Methods in Reading Class at School No. —.* Department of Education, Buffalo, N. Y., 1936.

DUNN, F. W. *Interest Factors in Primary Reading Material.* Contributions to Education, No. 113. Bureau of Publications, Teachers College, Columbia University, New York, 1921.

DURRELL, D. D. *Durrell Analysis of Reading Difficulty.* World Book Company, Yonkers-on-Hudson, N. Y., 1937.

DURRELL, D. D. "Tests and Corrective Procedures for Reading Disabilities." *Elementary English Review,* 12:91–95, April, 1935.

EAMES, T. "A Frequency Study of Physical Handicaps in Reading Disability and Unselected Groups." *Journal of Educational Research,* 29:1–5, September, 1935.

EAMES, T. AND PEABODY, R. W. "A Non-Reader Reads." *Journal of Educational Research,* 28:450–455, February, 1935.

FENDRICK, P. *Visual Characteristics of Poor Readers.* Contributions to Education, No. 656. Bureau of Publications, Teachers College, Columbia University, New York, 1935.

FERNALD, G. M. AND KELLER, H. "The Effect of Kinaesthetic Factors in the Development of Word Recognition in the Case of Non-Readers." *Journal of Educational Research,* 4:355–377, December, 1921.

FERNALD, G. M. AND KELLER, H. *On Certain Language Disabilities—Their Nature and Treatment.* Mental Measurement Monographs, Serial No. 11, August, 1936.

GARD, W. L. "The Influence of the Kindergarten on Achievement in Reading." *Educational Research Bulletin,* Ohio State University, pp. 135–138, April, 1924.

GARRETT, H. *Statistics in Psychology and Education.* Longmans, Green and Company, New York, 1926.

GATES, A. I. "An Experimental Evaluation of Reading Readiness Tests." *Elementary School Journal,* 39:497–508, March, 1939.

GATES, A. I. *The Improvement of Reading: A Program of Diagnostic and Remedial Methods.* Macmillan Company, New York, 1927. Also Revised Edition, 1935.

GATES, A. I. *Interest and Ability in Reading.* Macmillan Company, New York, 1930.

GATES, A. I. *New Methods in Primary Reading.* Bureau of Publications, Teachers College, Columbia University, New York, 1928.

GATES, A. I. *Gates Primary Reading Tests.* Manual. Bureau of Publications, Teachers College, Columbia University, New York, 1935.

GATES, A. I. "The Necessary Mental Age for Beginning Reading." *Elementary School Journal,* 37:497–508, March, 1937.

GATES, A. I. *The Psychology of Reading and Spelling with Special Reference to Disability.* Contributions to Education, No. 129. Bureau of Publications, Teachers College, Columbia University, New York, 1922.

GATES, A. I. "Viewpoints Underlying the Study of Reading Disability." *Elementary English Review,* 12:86–90, April, 1935.

GATES, A. I.; BATCHELDER, M. I.; AND BETZNER, J. "A Modern Systematic versus an Opportunistic Method of Teaching: An Experimental Study." *Teachers College Record*, 27:679–700, April, 1926.

GATES, A. I. AND BENNETT, C. C. *Reversal Tendencies in Reading*. Bureau of Publications, Teachers College, Columbia University, New York, 1933.

GATES, A. I. AND BOND, G. "Reading Readiness: A Study of Factors Determining Success and Failure in Beginning Reading." *Teachers College Record*, 37:679–685, May, 1936.

GATES, A. I.; BOND, G.; AND RUSSELL, D. *Methods of Determining Reading Readiness*. Bureau of Publications, Teachers College, Columbia University, New York, 1939.

GATES, A. I., AND HUBER, M. B. *The Work-Play Books*, Primer, Preparatory Book, and First Grade Manual. The Macmillan Company, New York, 1930.

GATES, A. I.; PEARDON, C.; AND SARTORIUS, I. "Studies of Children's Interests in Reading." *Elementary School Journal*, 31:656–670, May, 1931.

GATES, A. I. AND RUSSELL, D. "The Effects of Delaying Beginning Reading a Half Year in the Case of Underprivileged Pupils with I. Q.'s 75–95." *Journal of Educational Research*, 32:321–328, January, 1939.

GRANT, A. "A Comparison of the Metropolitan Readiness Tests and the Pintner-Cunningham Primary Mental Test." *Elementary School Journal*, 38:118–26, October, 1937.

GRAY, W. S. "Need of Cooperation between Laboratory and Classroom." *Journal of Educational Research*, 29:484–485, February, 1936.

GRAY, W. S. "The Nature and Organization of Basic Instruction in Reading," *The Teaching of Reading: A Second Report. Thirty-sixth Yearbook*, Part I. National Society for the Study of Education, Public School Publishing Company, Bloomington, Ill., 1937.

GRAY, W. S., with the cooperation of KIBBE, D., LUCAS, L., AND MILLER, L. *Remedial Cases in Reading; Their Diagnosis and Treatment*. Supplementary Educational Monographs No. 22. Department of Education, University of Chicago, Chicago, 1922.

GROSS, A. "A Preprimer Vocabulary Study." *Elementary School Journal*, 35:48–56, September, 1934.

HARRISON, M. *Reading Readiness*. Houghton Mifflin Company, Boston, 1936.

HECK, A. O. *Administration of Pupil Personnel*. Ginn and Company, New York, 1929.

HENDERSON, B. M. "Parental Attitudes toward First-Grade Achievement." *Understanding the Child*, 7:21–25, October, 1938.

HILDRETH, G. "Reversals in Reading and Writing." *Journal of Educational Psychology*, 24:1–20, January, 1934.

HILDRETH, G. AND GRIFFITHS, N. L. *Metropolitan Readiness Tests*. World Book Company, Yonkers-on-Hudson, N. Y., 1933.

HILLIARD, G. J. AND TROXELL, E. "Informational Background as a Factor in Reading Readiness and Reading Progress." *Elementary School Journal*, 38:255–263, December, 1937.

HOOPER, L. "What about School Failures?" *Elementary School Journal*, 36:349–53, January, 1936.

HORN, E., AND ASHBAUGH, E. *Progress in Spelling, Grades One to Four*. J. B. Lippincott Company, Philadelphia, 1935.

HUBBER, M. B. *The Influence of Intelligence upon Children's Reading Interests*. Contributions to Education, No. 312. Bureau of Publications, Teachers College, Columbia University, New York, 1928.

HULL, C. L. *Aptitude Testing*. World Book Company, Yonkers-on-Hudson, N. Y., 1928.

JUDD, C. H. AND BUSWELL, G. T. *Silent Reading: A Study of the Various Types*. Supplementary Educational Monographs, No. 23. University of Chicago, Chicago, November, 1922.

KELLEY, T. AND SHEN, E. "General Statistical Principles," *The Foundations of Experimental Psychology*. Clark University Press, Worcester, Mass., 1929.

LADD, M. *The Relation of Social, Economic, and Personal Characteristics to Reading Ability*. Contributions to Education, No. 582. Bureau of Publications, Teachers College, Columbia University, New York, 1933.

LEE, D. *The Importance of Reading for Achieving in Grades Four, Five, and Six*. Contributions to Education, No. 556. Bureau of Publications, Teachers College, Columbia University, New York, 1933.

LEE, J. M. AND CLARK, W. W. *Reading Readiness Tests and Manual*. Southern California School Book Depository, Hollywood, Cal., 1931.

LINDQUIST, E. "The Significance of a Difference between 'Matched' Groups." *Journal of Educational Psychology*, 22:197–204, March, 1931.

LIPPMAN, H. S. "Certain Behavior Responses in Early Infancy," *Journal of Genetic Psychology*, 34:424–440, September, 1927.

MCCALL, W. *How to Experiment in Education*. Macmillan Company, New York, 1923.

MCKEE, P. "Problems of Research: An Evaluation," *Research Problems in Reading in the Elementary School*. Fourth Annual Research Bulletin of the National Conference on Research in Elementary School English. Detroit, Michigan, 1936.

MEEK, L. H. *Study of Learning and Retention in Young Children*. Contributions to Education, No. 164. Bureau of Publications, Teachers College, Columbia University, New York, 1925.

MONROE, M. *Children Who Cannot Read: The Analysis of Reading Disabilities and the Use of Diagnostic Tests in the Instruction of Retarded Readers*. University of Chicago Press, Chicago, 1932.

MONROE, M. "Reading Aptitude Tests for the Prediction of Success and Failure in Beginning Reading." *Education*, 56:7–14, September, 1935.

Monroe, M. and Backus, B. *Remedial Reading.* Houghton Mifflin Company, Boston, 1937.

Morphett, M. and Washburne, C. "When Should Children Begin to Read?" *Elementary School Journal,* 31:496–503, March, 1931.

Mort, P. and Featherstone, W. *Entrance and Promotion Practices in City School Systems: Standards and Accounting Procedures.* Bureau of Publications, Teachers College, Columbia University, New York, 1932.

Mosher, R. M. "Some Results of Teaching Beginners by the Look-and-Say Method." *Journal of Educational Psychology,* 19:185–193, March, 1928.

National Committee on Reading. *The Twenty-Fourth Yearbook of the National Society for the Study of Education,* Part I. Public School Publishing Company, Bloomington, Ill., 1925.

National Committee on Reading. *The Thirty-Sixth Yearbook of the National Society for the Study of Education,* Part I. Public School Publishing Company, Bloomington, Ill., 1937.

Orton, S. T. "Specific Reading Disability—Strephosymbolia." *Journal of the American Medical Association,* 90:1095–1099, April, 1928.

Otis, A. *Otis Group Intelligence Scale, Primary Examination: Form A.* World Book Company, Yonkers-on-Hudson, N. Y., 1920.

Otto, H. J. "Implications for Administration and Teaching Growing Out of Pupil Failures in First Grade." *Elementary School Journal,* 33:25–32, September, 1932.

Percival, Walter P. "A Study of the Causes and Subjects of School Failure." Unpublished Doctor's Dissertation. Teachers College, Columbia University, New York, 1926.

Phillips, Arthur, "The Clinical Examination and Diagnostic Teaching of Cases at the Psychological Clinic of the University of Pennsylvania," *Psychological Clinic,* 19:169–200, November, 1930.

Pintner, R. and Cunningham, B. *The Pintner-Cunningham Primary Mental Test.* World Book Company, Yonkers-on-Hudson, N. Y., 1928.

Pugsley, C. A. "Reducing and Handling Student Failures." *School Board Journal,* 86:18–20, March, 1933.

Report of the Survey of the Schools of Chicago, Illinois. Summary of Findings and Recommendations. Bureau of Publications, Teachers College, Columbia University, New York, 1932.

Report of the Survey of the Schools of Evansville, Indiana. Unpublished Manuscript, 1935.

Report of the Survey of the Schools of Newburgh, New York. Made by the Institute of Educational Research, Division of Field Studies. Bureau of Publications, Teachers College, Columbia University, New York, 1929.

Research Committee. "The Prediction Value of the Lee-Clark Reading Readiness Test as Used in the Buffalo Public Schools." *Yearbook of the Buffalo Elementary School Principals Association,* Buffalo, N. Y., 1937.

Research Division of the National Education Association. *Better

Reading Instruction: A Survey of Research and Successful Practice. National Education Association, *Research Bulletin*, Vol. 13, Washington, D. C., November, 1935.

RUDISILL, M. "Selection of Preprimers and Primers—A Vocabulary Analysis." *Elementary School Journal,* 38:683–693 and 38:767–775, May and June, 1938.

STONE, C. *Better Primary Reading.* Webster Publishing Company, St. Louis, Mo., 1936.

STANGER, M. AND DONAHUE, E. *Prediction and Prevention of Reading Difficulties.* Oxford University Press, New York, 1937.

SMITH, N. *American Reading Instruction.* Silver, Burdett and Company, New York, 1934.

SMITH, N. "An Experiment to Determine the Effectiveness of Practice Tests in Teaching Beginning Reading." *Journal of Educational Research,* 7:213–228, March, 1923.

SMITH, N. "Matching Ability as a Factor in First Grade Reading." *Journal of Educational Psychology,* 19:560–571, November, 1928.

Survey of the Pasadena City Schools. Compiled and Published by the California Taxpayers Association, 1931.

TEEGARTEN, L. "Tests for the Tendency to Reversal in Reading." *Journal of Educational Research,* 27:81–97, October, 1933.

TERMAN, L. *The Measurement of Intelligence.* Houghton Mifflin Company, Boston, 1916.

THOMPSON, H. *An Experimental Study of the Beginning Reading of Deaf Mutes.* Contributions to Education No. 254. Bureau of Publications, Teachers College, Columbia University, New York, 1927.

THOMSON, J. L. "Big Gains from Postponed Reading." *Journal of Education,* 117:445–6, October, 1934.

UPDEGRAFF, R. "Ocular Dominance in Young Children." *Journal of Experimental Psychology,* 15:758–766, 1932.

VAN WAGENEN, M. J. *Reading Readiness Tests.* Educational Test Bureau, Minneapolis, Minn., 1932.

WATERS, D. "Prereading Experience." *Education,* 44:308, January, 1934.

WELLMAN, B. "The Development of Motor Coordination in Young Children." *University of Iowa Studies: Studies in Child Welfare,* Vol. 3, 1926.

WILKS, S. "The Standard Error of the Means of 'Matched' Samples." *Journal of Educational Psychology,* 22:205–208, March, 1931.

WILSON, F.; FLEMMING, C.; BURKE, A.; AND GARRISON, C. "Reading Progress in Kindergarten and Primary Grades." *Elementary School Journal,* 38:442–449, February, 1938.

WOODS, E. I. "A Study of the Entering B1 Children in the Los Angeles City Schools." *Journal of Educational Research,* 21:9–19, September, 1937.

VITA

HOWARD THOMAS DUNKLIN was born July 3, 1899, in the city of Buffalo, New York. He received the Bachelor of Arts Degree from Canisius College, Buffalo, in 1921. The Master of Arts Degree was conferred upon him in 1929 by the University of Buffalo. At Columbia University, his graduate study was in the fields of Psychology and Education.